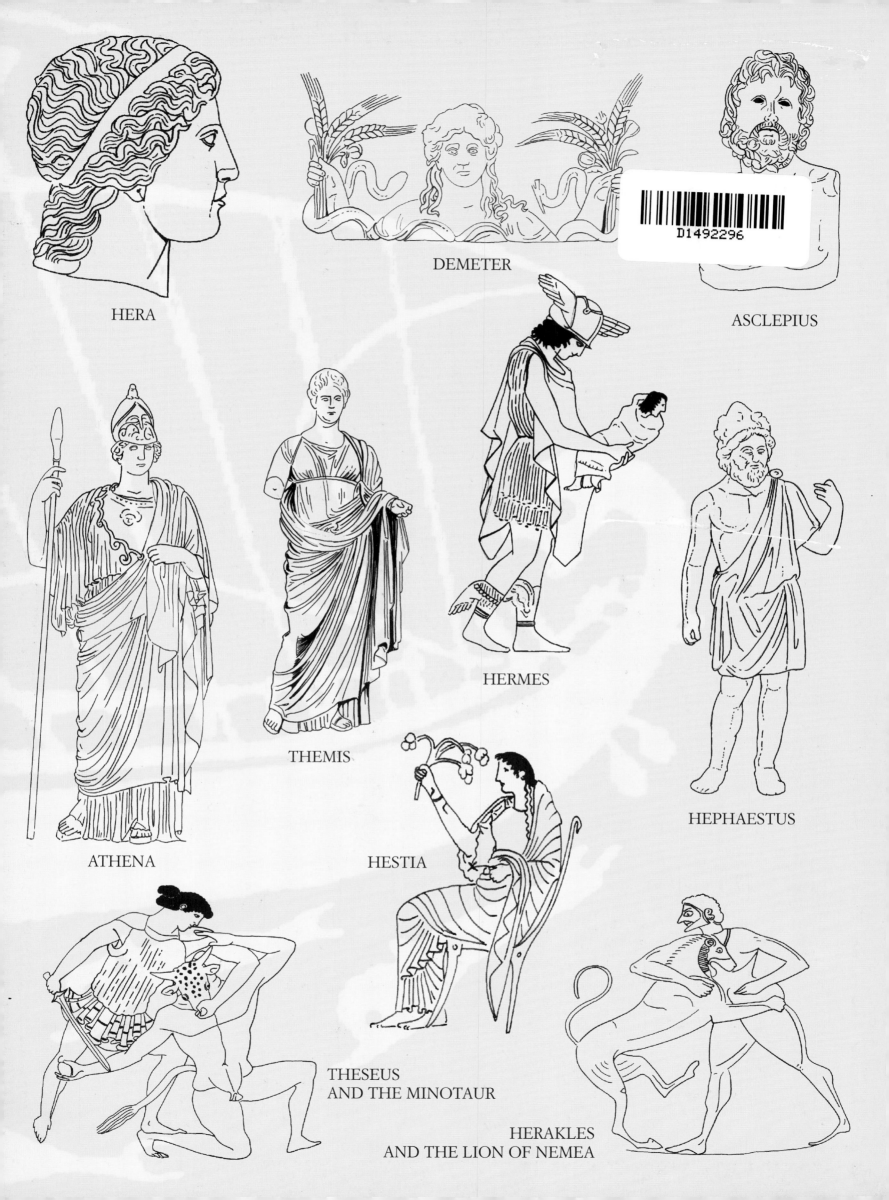

HERA

DEMETER

ASCLEPIUS

HERMES

ATHENA

THEMIS

HESTIA

HEPHAESTUS

THESEUS
AND THE MINOTAUR

HERAKLES
AND THE LION OF NEMEA

This edition published by
Macdonald Young Books,
an imprint of Wayland Publishers Ltd
61 Western Road
Hove, East Sussex BN3 1JD

You can find
Macdonald Young Books
on the internet at
http://www.wayland.co.uk

ISBN 0 7500 2408 9

A catalogue record for this book
is available from the British Library

The Atlas of Ancient Greece and Ancient Rome
was created and produced by McRae Books,
via de' Rustici, 5 – Florence (Italy)
E-mail mcrae@tin.it

Text Piero Bardi
Main illustrations Matteo Chesi, Ferruccio
Cucchiarini, Paola Ravaglia, Ivan Stalio
Other illustrations Alessandro Bartolozzi, Alessandro
Cantucci, Lorenzo Cecchi, Rosa Gaudenzi, Paola
Holguín, Francesco Micheli, Andrea Morandi,
Antonella Pastorelli, Giacomo Soriani
Translation Anne McRae
Graphic Design Marco Nardi
Colour separations R.A.F., Florence (Italy)

Printed in Italy by Grafiche Editoriali Padane

THE ATLAS OF ANCIENT
GREECE
AND ANCIENT
ROME

Text by Piero Bardi

Illustrations by Matteo Chesi, Ferruccio
Cucchiarini, Paola Ravaglia, Ivan Stalio

Alessandro Bartolozzi, Alessandro Cantucci, Lorenzo Cecchi,
Rosa Gaudenzi, Paola Holguín, Francesco Micheli, Andrea
Morandi, Antonella Pastorelli, Giacomo Soriani

Macdonald Young Books

The Acropolis in Athens
Greek towns had a centrally located, well defended district containing the main religious and civic buildings. This area was called the acropolis. The illustration shows a reconstruction of the Athenian Acropolis, built in the second half of the 5th century.

The Parthenon. The chief temple of Athena, goddess of the city. It was built under the guidance of Pericles by the architects Ictinus and Callicrates, with the sculptor Phidias. It dates from 447–432 BC.

Votive statue from Sparta playing the double pipes

Erechtheum. This temple of Athena is one of the most beautiful examples of Ionic architecture ever built. It has a special caryatid porch (see p. 29).

Chalkotheke. Bronze votive offerings were kept here.

Sanctuary of the bear goddess Artemis Brauronia. Votive offerings, including beautifully carved bears, were kept here.

Temple of Athena Nike. The temple to the goddess of victory, Nike, was built in 449 BC to celebrate the peace with Persia.

House of the Arrephoroi. Four young girls of noble birth lived here. They wove and carried the peplos for Athena (see pp. 18–19) and performed other mysterious duties in her honour.

Thick defence walls.

Colossal bronze statue of Athena in military dress. The point of her lance is said to have guided ships into the port of Athens.

The Propylaea. The monumental gateway to the sacred buildings within. It was designed by Mnesicles in the 5th century BC.

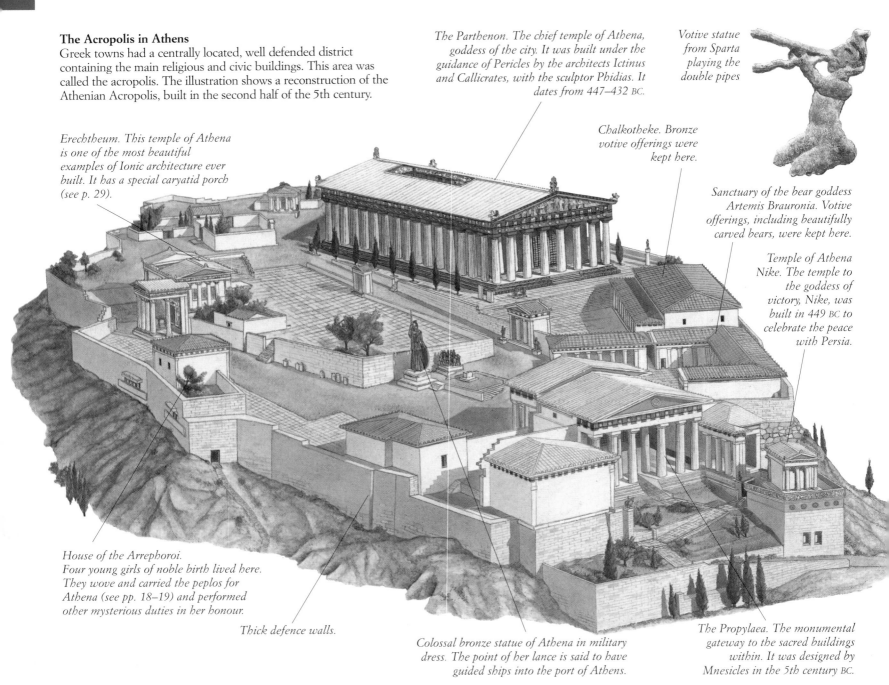

Contents

Introduction

Beyond the Classical World
The influence of Greece and Rome went well beyond the frontiers of their city-states or Empire. Through trade and contact of various types, they spread their cultures from the Mediterranean to Europe, Asia and Africa. Even now, long after the demise of these civilizations, their influence is still felt, in our languages, systems of government, art, architecture and scientific discovery.

The Classical World covers a period of well over a thousand years, from the rise of city-states in Greece in the 8th century BC to the fall of the Roman Empire in the West in AD 476. Geographically, the Classical World is focused around the Mediterranean Sea, although the Roman Empire takes us west as far as England and east to the Persian Gulf. The ancestors of the Greeks were Indo-Europeans who entered Greece from the north around 1900 BC. They lived alongside the Minoans for many centuries, before giving rise to the Mycenaean civilization which ended in the 12th century BC. After a break of around 300 years, during which the knowledge of writing was somehow lost, Greece gave birth to one of the most astonishing civilizations the world has ever known – Classical Greece. Despite its achievements, it flourished briefly, peaking in the 5th century BC before succumbing to Alexander the Great two centuries later. Just a short distance away, across the Adriatic Sea in Italy, the Etruscan civilization was in full bloom. Contact with the Etruscans and Greeks encouraged the Latin people to raise Rome from a wayside village to a great city, capital of a huge Empire governing over millions of people. The year 476 marks not only the fall of the Western Empire but also the beginning of European history, as the centres of power in Europe moved away from the Mediterranean to northern Europe.

Greek and Roman coins. Greek city-states and Roman emperors minted many new coins. They were often decorated with symbols typical of the local area.

Both the Romans and Greeks were religious peoples. This tiny statue comes from the sanctuary of Artemis at Sparta.

The Baths of Caracalla in Rome
Thermal baths were one of the most characteristic signs of Roman civilization. Bath complexes have been found in every province of the Empire. There were at least ten monumental baths in the city of Rome. The illustration shows a reconstruction of the Baths of Caracalla. They could accommodate up to 1,600 bathers at a time. Opened in AD 217, they stayed in use until the 6th century when invading Gauls damaged the aqueducts which carried waters to the baths.

Mythology
The Greeks and Romans have left us a rich store of myths and legends about their gods and heroes. In the vase painting above, Herakles (Roman Hercules) journeys in a pot boat to the Garden of Hesperides.

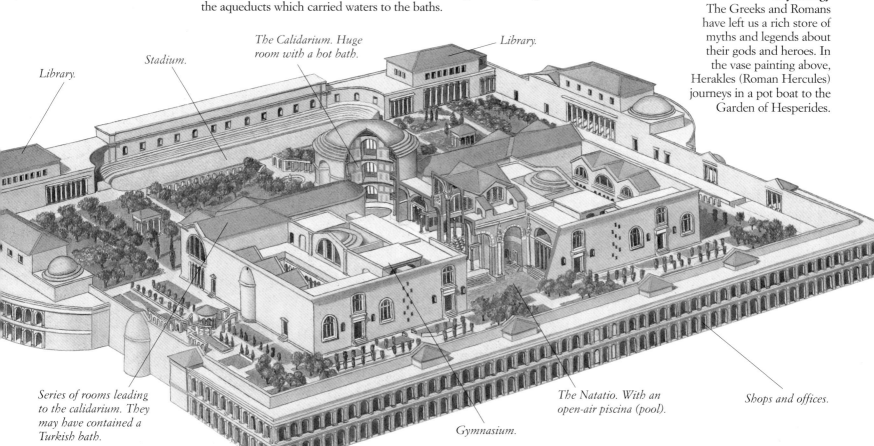

Library.

Stadium.

The Calidarium. Huge room with a hot bath.

Library.

Series of rooms leading to the calidarium. They may have contained a Turkish bath.

Gymnasium.

The Natatio. With an open-air piscina (pool).

Shops and offices.

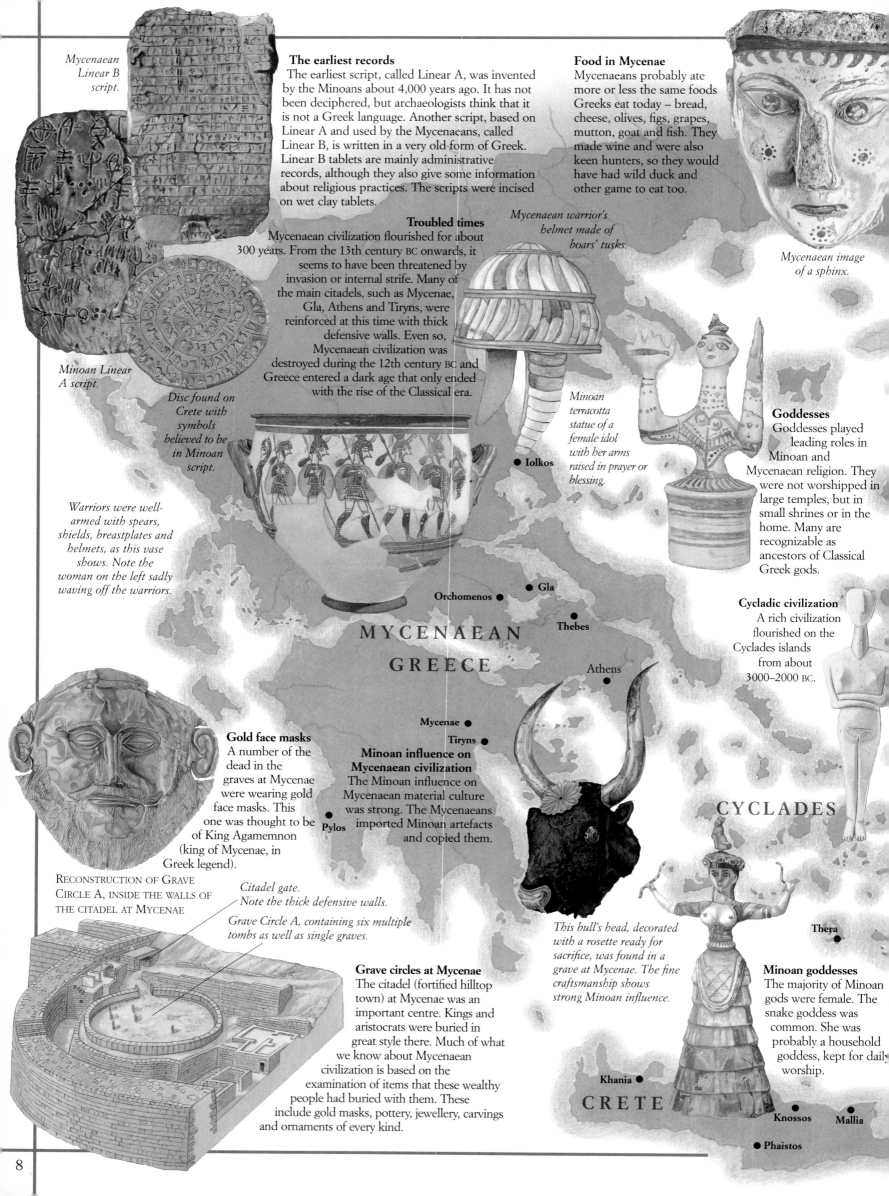

Mycenaean Linear B script.

The earliest records
The earliest script, called Linear A, was invented by the Minoans about 4,000 years ago. It has not been deciphered, but archaeologists think that it is not a Greek language. Another script, based on Linear A and used by the Mycenaeans, called Linear B, is written in a very old form of Greek. Linear B tablets are mainly administrative records, although they also give some information about religious practices. The scripts were incised on wet clay tablets.

Food in Mycenae
Mycenaeans probably ate more or less the same foods Greeks eat today – bread, cheese, olives, figs, grapes, mutton, goat and fish. They made wine and were also keen hunters, so they would have had wild duck and other game to eat too.

Mycenaean image of a sphinx.

Minoan Linear A script.

Disc found on Crete with symbols believed to be in Minoan script.

Troubled times
Mycenaean civilization flourished for about 300 years. From the 13th century BC onwards, it seems to have been threatened by invasion or internal strife. Many of the main citadels, such as Mycenae, Gla, Athens and Tiryns, were reinforced at this time with thick defensive walls. Even so, Mycenaean civilization was destroyed during the 12th century BC and Greece entered a dark age that only ended with the rise of the Classical era.

Mycenaean warrior's helmet made of boars' tusks.

Minoan terracotta statue of a female idol with her arms raised in prayer or blessing.

Goddesses
Goddesses played leading roles in Minoan and Mycenaean religion. They were not worshipped in large temples, but in small shrines or in the home. Many are recognizable as ancestors of Classical Greek gods.

Warriors were well-armed with spears, shields, breastplates and helmets, as this vase shows. Note the woman on the left sadly waving off the warriors.

● **Iolkos**

● **Gla**
Orchomenos ●

● **Thebes**

MYCENAEAN
GREECE

Cycladic civilization
A rich civilization flourished on the Cyclades islands from about 3000–2000 BC.

Athens ●

Gold face masks
A number of the dead in the graves at Mycenae were wearing gold face masks. This one was thought to be of King Agamemnon (king of Mycenae, in Greek legend).

Mycenae ●

Tiryns ●

Minoan influence on Mycenaean civilization
The Minoan influence on Mycenaean material culture was strong. The Mycenaeans imported Minoan artefacts and copied them.

Pylos ●

RECONSTRUCTION OF GRAVE CIRCLE A, INSIDE THE WALLS OF THE CITADEL AT MYCENAE

Citadel gate. Note the thick defensive walls.

Grave Circle A, containing six multiple tombs as well as single graves.

CYCLADES

Grave circles at Mycenae
The citadel (fortified hilltop town) at Mycenae was an important centre. Kings and aristocrats were buried in great style there. Much of what we know about Mycenaean civilization is based on the examination of items that these wealthy people had buried with them. These include gold masks, pottery, jewellery, carvings and ornaments of every kind.

This bull's head, decorated with a rosette ready for sacrifice, was found in a grave at Mycenae. The fine craftsmanship shows strong Minoan influence.

Thera ●

Minoan goddesses
The majority of Minoan gods were female. The snake goddess was common. She was probably a household goddess, kept for daily worship.

Khania ●

CRETE

Knossos ● ● **Mallia**

● **Phaistos**

The Minoan double-axe

The double-axe was an important religious emblem for Minoans. Some basement rooms of the palace of Knossos have pillars decorated with double-axe designs. It was probably the symbol of a Minoan god – some have suggested the sky god. This engraved gold axe was found in a sacred cave in Crete.

The Fisherman, from the island of Thera.

Wall paintings

Minoan artists painted stunningly beautiful frescoes, a few of which have survived. They are done in a naturalistic style and provide us with useful information about Minoan lifestyles, clothing, religious ceremonies, boats and general outlook.

Bull-leaping

The mysterious bull-leaping ceremony was probably performed by professional acrobats. It is not known whether this dangerous sport was done for entertainment or as part of a religious ceremony.

Minoans and Mycenaeans

The Classical World of ancient Greece and Rome grew over the remains of two earlier civilizations that flourished in the same area many centuries earlier. The Minoan civilization prospered on the Mediterranean island of Crete from about 2000 BC. The Minoans, named after the legendary Cretan king Minos, originally came from the Middle East. They built huge palaces from which kings ruled over the surrounding countryside, organizing agriculture and trade. They had their own written script and were highly skilled craftspeople. The Minoan palaces, and the civilization itself, were destroyed around 1450 BC, either by earthquake or enemy attack.

The Mycenaeans, who replaced the Minoans as the dominant power in the region, arrived in Greece from the north. Mycenaean Greece consisted of a number of small kingdoms, each centred on a palace or citadel. The Mycenaeans were a warlike people, but they were also enterprising traders, able administrators and talented craftspeople. They took control of Crete around 1450 BC, borrowing heavily from the earlier Minoans. Mycenaean civilization continued into the 12th century BC, when the last of its palaces were sacked or abandoned. The famous Greek epic poems, the *Iliad* and the *Odyssey*, by Homer, may refer to events in Mycenaean history.

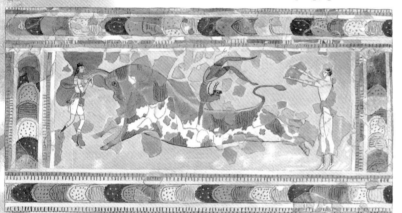

Fragment of a fresco showing bull-leaping, from the palace of Knossos. The white figures are women and the red leaping figure is a man.

The palace of Knossos

Knossos was the largest of the Cretan palaces. It was built around 2000 BC over the ruins of earlier human settlements. It covered just under a hectare and was arranged around a rectangular courtyard. The royal apartments and other living quarters were on the upper floors. They were decorated with frescoes of goddesses, religious and sporting ceremonies, animals, plants and geometrical designs, all of astonishing beauty. The ground floor and basement were used as storerooms for oil, wine and other farm products, and workshops where skilled craftspeople produced pottery, jewellery, carvings and metalwork. Clay tablets, in Mycenaean script from the 14th century BC, record that at that time almost 4,300 people were receiving rations from the palace and that it controlled flocks of about 80,000 sheep. The palace had efficient drains and clay pipes carried water to the bathrooms. Smaller palaces have been discovered at Mallia, Phaistos, Zakto, Khania and on the island of Thera.

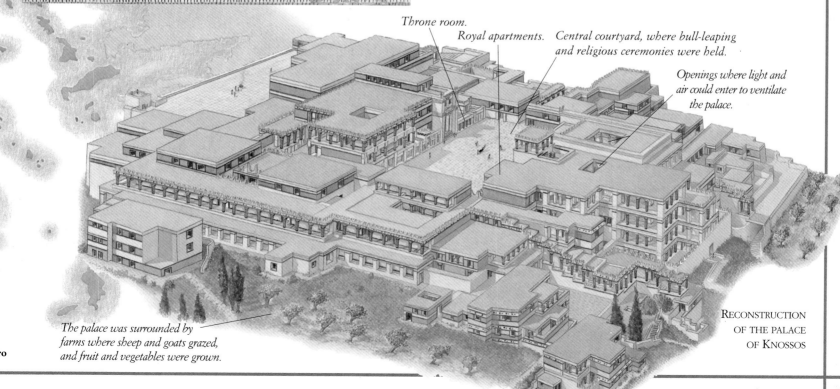

Throne room.

Royal apartments.

Central courtyard, where bull-leaping and religious ceremonies were held.

Openings where light and air could enter to ventilate the palace.

The palace was surrounded by farms where sheep and goats grazed, and fruit and vegetables were grown.

akro

RECONSTRUCTION OF THE PALACE OF KNOSSOS

The Emergence of City-States

Little is known of the four centuries following the end of Mycenaean civilization. Historians have sometimes called this time, from the 11th–8th centuries BC, the 'Dark Ages', although recent discoveries by archaeologists have shown that some rich and well-organized cities existed even then. Most historians agree that it was a period of unrest and migration. New peoples from the north, known as Dorians, are thought to have settled in Greece at this time. Gradually things settled down, and we know that by the 8th century BC growing towns and the countryside surrounding them were ruled by aristocratic families or military leaders. These small, self-governing communities are known as *poleis,* or city-states. By about 700 BC almost all of Greece was divided into independent *poleis*. Over the centuries most of them developed more democratic forms of government. In Classical times, a typical *polis* (city-state) was composed of citizens (adult males), citizens without political rights (women and children of male citizens), and non-citizens (foreigners and slaves). It was governed by elected male citizens who met in the *agora* (marketplace) to decide how the *polis* should be run. The *polis* is a unique feature of Greek civilization.

Clay centaur (half man, half horse) found in the tombs at Lefkandi.

Lefkandi
Excavations at Lefkandi in central Greece have uncovered the tombs of a man and woman who were buried in great luxury in about 950 BC. The graves are magnificent and contain items of beauty and value, many of which were imported from abroad. Archaeologists now know that at least one wealthy and powerful city existed during the so-called Dark Ages. There may have been others.

Pottery in Archaic times
The earliest Greek vases were decorated with geometric patterns, including bands of zigzags, triangles and meanders. New patterns developed slowly and, during the 9th-8th centuries BC, figures of animals and people began to reappear. At first they were simple and stylized figures of animals, or mourners on funeral vases. Many show the influence of other civilizations, suggesting that the Greeks were once again trading with neighbouring peoples.

1. Geometric vase. 8th century BC.
2. Athenian vase from 730 BC with figures of people and horses.
3. Tiny perfume bottle made at Corinth. Bottles like this were used to export perfumed oil. The decoration shows the influence of people from the Near East.
4. Late-Mycenaean vase from Cyprus. Mycenaean art continued on some outlying islands after the end of the civilization.

Below: scene from a funeral vase showing a dead woman on her bier surrounded by mourners. The vase stands 1.55 metres tall. It was used as a grave-marker in the cemetery of Athens.

Clay figure of a woman or goddess decorated in the same style as vases of the 8th century BC.

Funeral customs
Large vases were often used as grave markers, particularly in Athens. Rich people had a vase made and decorated showing scenes of mourning at their funerals. The vase was placed near the grave.

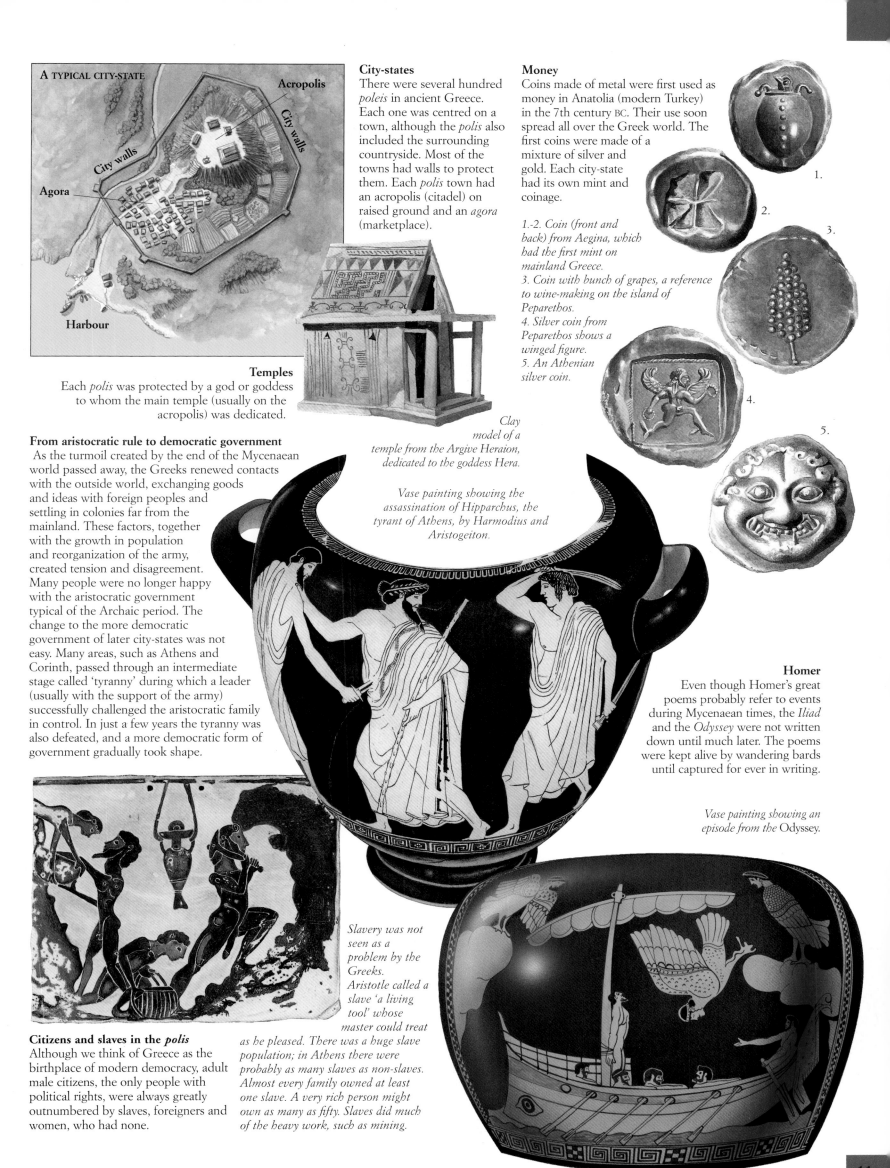

City-states

There were several hundred *poleis* in ancient Greece. Each one was centred on a town, although the *polis* also included the surrounding countryside. Most of the towns had walls to protect them. Each *polis* town had an acropolis (citadel) on raised ground and an *agora* (marketplace).

A TYPICAL CITY-STATE

Acropolis

City walls

City walls

Agora

Harbour

Money

Coins made of metal were first used as money in Anatolia (modern Turkey) in the 7th century BC. Their use soon spread all over the Greek world. The first coins were made of a mixture of silver and gold. Each city-state had its own mint and coinage.

1.-2. Coin (front and back) from Aegina, which had the first mint on mainland Greece.
3. Coin with bunch of grapes, a reference to wine-making on the island of Peparethos.
4. Silver coin from Peparethos shows a winged figure.
5. An Athenian silver coin.

1.

2.

3.

4.

5.

Temples

Each *polis* was protected by a god or goddess to whom the main temple (usually on the acropolis) was dedicated.

Clay model of a temple from the Argive Heraion, dedicated to the goddess Hera.

From aristocratic rule to democratic government

As the turmoil created by the end of the Mycenaean world passed away, the Greeks renewed contacts with the outside world, exchanging goods and ideas with foreign peoples and settling in colonies far from the mainland. These factors, together with the growth in population and reorganization of the army, created tension and disagreement. Many people were no longer happy with the aristocratic government typical of the Archaic period. The change to the more democratic government of later city-states was not easy. Many areas, such as Athens and Corinth, passed through an intermediate stage called 'tyranny' during which a leader (usually with the support of the army) successfully challenged the aristocratic family in control. In just a few years the tyranny was also defeated, and a more democratic form of government gradually took shape.

Vase painting showing the assassination of Hipparchus, the tyrant of Athens, by Harmodius and Aristogeiton.

Homer

Even though Homer's great poems probably refer to events during Mycenaean times, the *Iliad* and the *Odyssey* were not written down until much later. The poems were kept alive by wandering bards until captured for ever in writing.

Vase painting showing an episode from the Odyssey.

Slavery was not seen as a problem by the Greeks. Aristotle called a slave 'a living tool' whose master could treat as he pleased. There was a huge slave population; in Athens there were probably as many slaves as non-slaves. Almost every family owned at least one slave. A very rich person might own as many as fifty. Slaves did much of the heavy work, such as mining.

Citizens and slaves in the *polis*

Although we think of Greece as the birthplace of modern democracy, adult male citizens, the only people with political rights, were always greatly outnumbered by slaves, foreigners and women, who had none.

Sparta and Athens

The many city-states were all governed in different ways. We know more about Athens than any of the other *poleis* because the Athenians left so many records. We also know quite a lot about the *polis* of Sparta, in the south, which was another large and powerful city-state. The two *poleis* were run on very different, almost opposing principles. At its height in the mid-5th century BC, Athens was a democratic state (at least in ancient terms), run by elected male citizens. Freedom, tolerance and intellectual curiosity were highly esteemed qualities. Sparta was governed by military leaders. Discipline, loyalty and self-denial were the chief Spartan virtues. The two fought for many years in the Peloponnesian War (431–404 BC), dividing the support of the other Greek *poleis* between them. Sparta won in the end, although the war was so devastating that neither side ever really recovered.

This awesome bronze statue of a Spartan warrior was carved by an unknown sculptor some 2,500 years ago.

Sport
Even more emphasis was placed on physical training and sporting ability among the warlike Spartan people than in the other city-states.

A military life
At the age of seven all Spartan boy citizens were taken from their families to begin their long military training. They did not return to family life until they were thirty years old. Even then, Spartan males were expected to continue military training and to spend their spare time with other soldiers rather than at home with their wives and children.

The Spartan state
Sparta became the most efficient military power in Greece. Spartan males dedicated all their time and energy to the army. They were kept by slaves owned by the state, called 'helots', who were the original inhabitants of the area. The helots, the vast majority of the population, did all the hard work. Trade and commerce were carried out by another group, called *perioikoi* (neighbours), who were not citizens but were not as badly treated as the helots.

Lycurgus – 'founding father'
Sparta had a unique form of government. It was controlled by two kings from aristocratic families who governed by military rule. There was also an assembly of Spartan citizens, although their decisions could be overruled at any time by the kings and their aristocratic council. Traditionally, it was believed that this form of government was established by a man called Lycurgus. Ancient scholars thought that he lived in about 1,000 BC when Sparta was settled by the Doric invaders who became the Spartans. Modern historians are not even sure that he existed; if so, he probably lived in the 7th century BC.

Spartan girls were also given rigorous physical educations so that they could produce strong Spartan babies.

Vase painting showing Spartan wrestlers engaged in violent combat.

This small statue comes from the sanctuary of Artemis Orthia in Sparta. Statues like this were left as offerings to the goddess Artemis. The sanctuary was also used in ceremonies where Spartan boys were ritually flogged; this was supposed to increase their courage as future soldiers.

Composition of society in Athens and Sparta
The two triangular graphs represent the composition of society in Athens and Sparta. As they show, only a small percentage of the inhabitants of both *poleis* were citizens. However, the situation was a little better in Athens than in Sparta.

Spartan citizens
By law the only people eligible for citizenship in Sparta were the direct descendents of the original Doric settlers. They kept themselves separate from the rest of the population in a closed aristocratic society. Because of this, there were never more than about 6,000–7,000 male citizens in Sparta (compared with up to 40,000 in Athens).

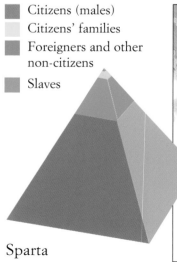

Sparta

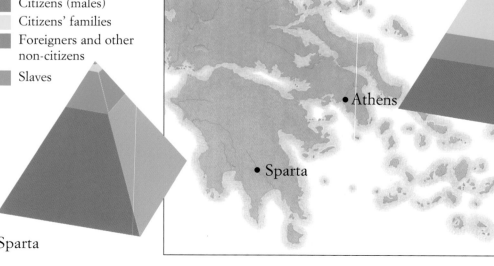

Athens

MAP SHOWING THE LOCATION OF SPARTA AND ATHENS

- Citizens (males)
- Citizens' families
- Foreigners and other non-citizens
- Slaves

• Athens

• Sparta

Athenian democracy

In Athens the change from aristocratic government to democracy took many years. Several names are associated with the reforms that led to democratic government. Early in the 6th century BC Solon introduced changes which limited the influence of the aristocracy and slightly increased the power of poorer citizens. At the end of the same century Cleisthenes brought in even more revolutionary reforms. He divided Attica (the city and countryside of Athens) into ten new tribes, each made up of *demes* (villages) from three geographical areas – City, Plains and Coast. Within the *demes* all male citizens had the same amount of power regardless of their family or income and all could participate in central government. The tribes contributed equal numbers of members to the new Council of Five Hundred, which prepared material for the Assembly to discuss and vote on. The Assembly was composed of up to 40,000 male citizens. 6,000 was the minimum number (quorum) when important decisions were to be voted on.

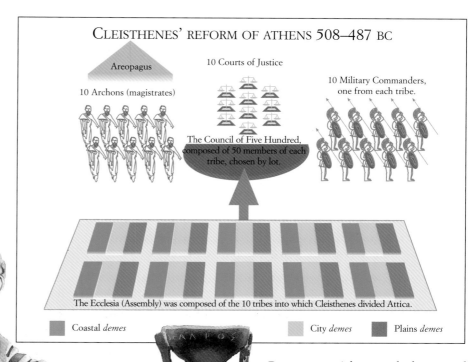

CLEISTHENES' REFORM OF ATHENS 508–487 BC

Areopagus

10 Archons (magistrates)

10 Courts of Justice

10 Military Commanders, one from each tribe.

The Council of Five Hundred, composed of 50 members of each tribe, chosen by lot.

The Ecclesia (Assembly) was composed of the 10 tribes into which Cleisthenes divided Attica.

Coastal *demes*   City *demes*   Plains *demes*

Bust of Demosthenes.

Demosthenes – the greatest orator

In democratic Athens the ability to speak well in public – to be an 'orator' – was well rewarded. Demosthenes (384–322 BC), robbed of his inheritance by unscrupulous guardians, rose to power nonetheless because of his skill as an orator. Although any citizen could speak at the Assembly of Athens, bad speakers were jeered at and shouted down. After much study and practise, Demosthenes became an influential statesman because he was able to put his case well in the Assembly. Many of his speeches were recorded; they provide valuable information on social, political and economic life in 4th century BC Athens.

Freedom of speech with time limitation

Clocks and watches were unknown in ancient Greece. The Greeks used a clepsydra or 'water clock' to measure the amount of time allowed to each speaker at a trial or public meeting.

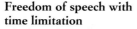

Two vases placed one above the other were used to measure the time allowed to public speakers.

Democracy in Athens was both more and less democratic than it is in Britain today. It was more democratic because the Assembly was relatively small and citizens had direct access to decision-making. On the other hand, it was less democratic because whole groups, including women and foreigners, were excluded.

The two bronze wheels (below) are public ballots. They were used by voters to condemn or acquit someone on trial. Wheels with solid axles, like the ones shown here, were for acquittal. If the axles were hollow, it meant that the defendant was condemned.

Bust of Pericles.

Pericles' Athens

Pericles (495–429 BC) was an important leader in Athens during its period of greatest power in the 440s and 430s BC. He was a brilliant politician, statesman and general. Under his leadership holders of public offices began to be paid. This was an important step forward in the democratic process because it gave poor citizens the opportunity to take part in government. Pericles was also responsible for rebuilding Athens after the damage caused during the Persian Wars. The port of Piraeus was enlarged, the city walls were extended and a magnificent building programme began on the Acropolis. The Parthenon and the other buildings still visible on the Acropolis today were begun under his guidance.

Ostracism

A political rival or unwanted member of the *polis* could be sent into exile for ten years by way of ostracism. The Assembly voted on whether a person should be sent away or not. These potsherds (pieces of pottery), or *ostraca* (right), list the names of men voted to be ostracised.

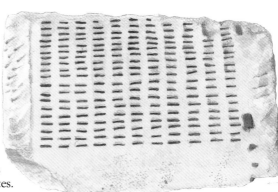

Appointment by lot

To ensure that rich or influential men could not buy votes and power, a system called appointment by lot was invented. Candidates for many positions were chosen at random from among all the citizens. The *kleroterion* (right) was used to extract the names of successful candidates.

Tiny terracotta figure, showing a woman kneading dough.

Daily Life

The family was the basic social unit in ancient Greece, just as it is in most parts of the world today. In wealthy homes men and women lived in separate parts of the house. The *gynaeceum*, or women's quarters, was reserved for female members of the family, their children and close female friends. Rich women lived secluded lives and rarely left the house unless going to a wedding, funeral or religious ceremony. When they did go out they were always accompanied by a male relative or slave. Women from poor families had more freedom; they had to leave the house to do the shopping, haul water and to work. Men of all classes spent most of their time away from the house and out of doors. Farmers tended their fields, and artisans and merchants plied their trades in and around the *agora*. Wealthy male citizens spent much of their time talking to others of their kind and deciding how the *polis* should be run.

Man moving a couch and table.

Women's work
Greek women led busy lives. Mothers, even wealthy ones, cared for their children themselves. Women were responsible for running the household; domestic chores took up a large amount of time and energy.

Furniture
Furniture was simple, light and kept to a minimum. Many items had more than one use; for example a dinner couch could double as a bed. Typical pieces of furniture included couches, tables, stools and many chests and trunks for storing clothing, blankets and linen.

Women working at a loom.

Weaving
Even in wealthy families where there were slaves and servants to do most of the heavy work, women were expected to keep themselves busy. Weaving and spinning were acceptable tasks; women wove and spun linen and wool into cloth and produced clothing for the whole family.

Inside the house
A typical house had a simple floor of flattened earth. Cookery pots, tools and utensils of every sort were hung on the walls. Many richer households had decorative wall-hangings or painted scenes.

Decorative spoons made of clay with animal heads.

This relief statue shows a woman putting linen away in a simple chest.

Children
Children lived with their mothers in the *gynaeceum*. Many had toys, including rattles, tops, hoops and tiny figures like the goose and rider shown here. At about age seven wealthy boys were sent to private schools where they learned to read, write and do sums. Girls stayed at home to learn domestic work. Only a few girls were taught to read and write. The children of very poor families or slaves worked from an early age.

Clothing
Both men and women wore long, flowing tunics that were often richly decorated with sprigs, spots and scrolls. In colder weather they wore a woollen garment over the top. They wore sandals or baggy, skin boots on their feet. Many women had elaborate hair-styles with curls and ribbons.

After dinner at a drinking party.

At night lighting was provided by oil lamps like the one shown here.

An ornate hand mirror.

Adult entertainment
Male members of the family often gave dinner parties for their friends. They reclined on couches, ate sumptuous meals, drank wine and were amused by female entertainers (this was not considered a respectable occupation for women). We know less about family meals and ladies' parties, but they were undoubtedly more sober affairs.

Beauty aids
Cosmetics were popular among Greek women. Many used make-up to lighten the colour of their skins, as well as perfume and elaborate hair-styles. They had special boxes for storing jewellery.

Wedding procession

The close-knit Greek family had clear-cut rituals regarding marriage. The bride passed from her father's family to her husband's. Before the ceremony and feast in her father's home, the bride took a special bath. At the feast she sat veiled and apart from the men with other women. Hymns were sung in honour of the god of marriage. After the feast she was taken in a procession to her husband's home. When she arrived, she was showered with dried fruit and nuts, symbols of fertility.

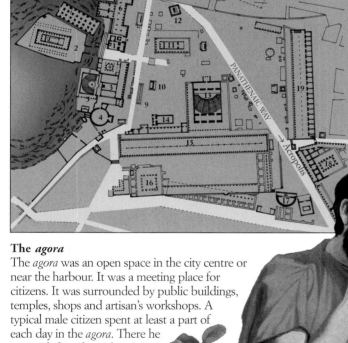

Small businesses in the *agora*

The *agora* was crowded with cobblers, fishmongers, potters, money-changers, barbers and many other craftspeople and traders. Most businesses were small, run by a family with perhaps one or two slaves.

Since wealthy women were not allowed to go out, the men or slaves did the daily shopping for food in the agora.

DIAGRAM OF THE *AGORA* IN ATHENS IN THE 2ND CENTURY AD

The barber's shop

Some shops in the *agora* were meeting places. The barber's shop was a favourite, and groups of men gathered there to discuss important issues or to gossip.

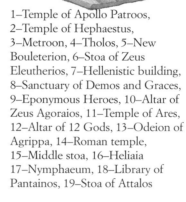

Having a haircut 2,500 years ago.

A Greek diet

Bread was one of the staple foods; a typical lunch would be bread dipped in a little wine, and a few figs and olives. Dinner in the evening was the main meal of the day. Fish was a common dish. Meat was expensive and was reserved for special occasions.

1–Temple of Apollo Patroos, 2–Temple of Hephaestus, 3–Metroon, 4–Tholos, 5–New Bouleterion, 6–Stoa of Zeus Eleutherios, 7–Hellenistic building, 8–Sanctuary of Demos and Graces, 9–Eponymous Heroes, 10–Altar of Zeus Agoraios, 11–Temple of Ares, 12–Altar of 12 Gods, 13–Odeion of Agrippa, 14–Roman temple, 15–Middle stoa, 16–Heliaia 17–Nymphaeum, 18–Library of Pantainos, 19–Stoa of Attalos

Monument to the Eponymous Heroes, in the agora, *Athens.*

The *agora*

The *agora* was an open space in the city centre or near the harbour. It was a meeting place for citizens. It was surrounded by public buildings, temples, shops and artisan's workshops. A typical male citizen spent at least a part of each day in the *agora*. There he met with friends, took part in political life and kept himself informed on what was going on. The Monument to Eponymous Heroes (right) was a public notice-board, where military call-ups were listed, and new laws and public honours announced.

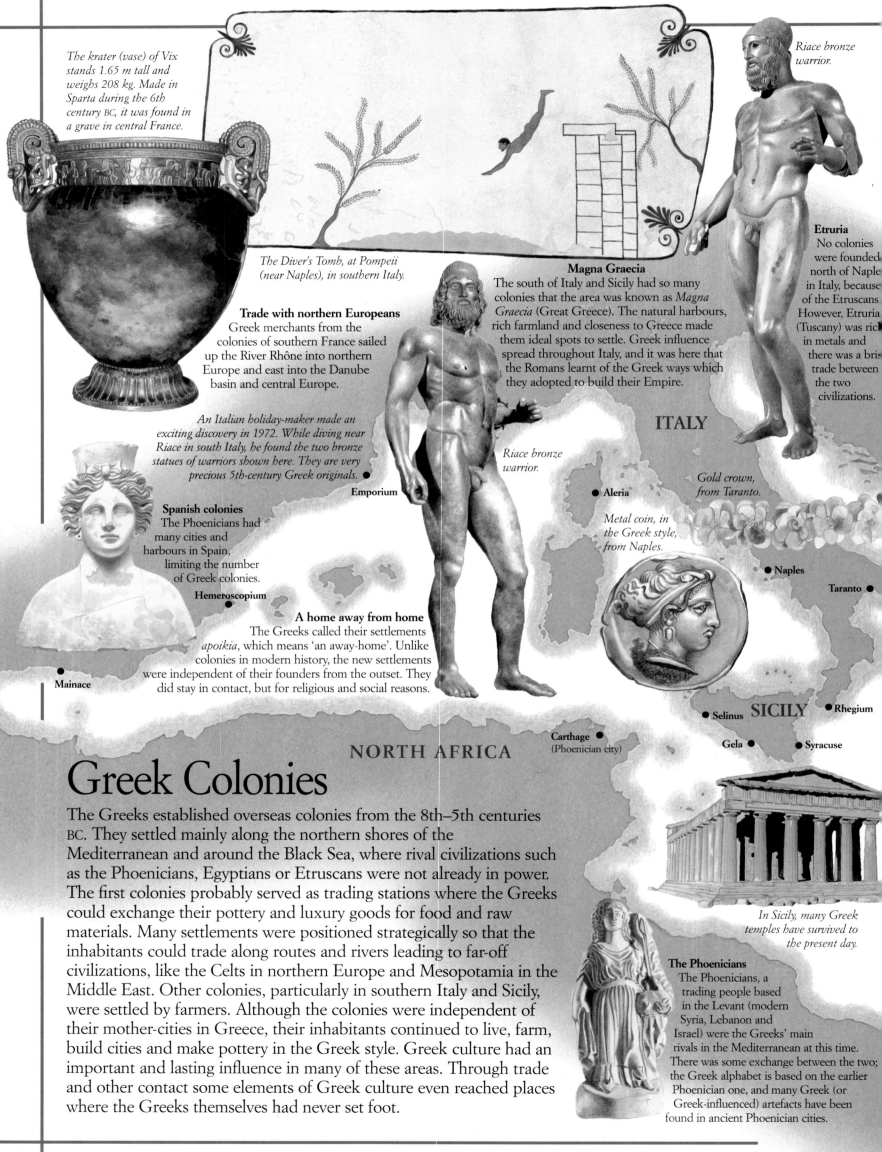

The krater (vase) of Vix stands 1.65 m tall and weighs 208 kg. Made in Sparta during the 6th century BC, it was found in a grave in central France.

The Diver's Tomb, at Pompeii (near Naples), in southern Italy.

Trade with northern Europeans
Greek merchants from the colonies of southern France sailed up the River Rhône into northern Europe and east into the Danube basin and central Europe.

An Italian holiday-maker made an exciting discovery in 1972. While diving near Riace in south Italy, he found the two bronze statues of warriors shown here. They are very precious 5th-century Greek originals.

Emporium

Spanish colonies
The Phoenicians had many cities and harbours in Spain, limiting the number of Greek colonies.

Hemeroscopium

A home away from home
The Greeks called their settlements *apoikia*, which means 'an away-home'. Unlike colonies in modern history, the new settlements were independent of their founders from the outset. They did stay in contact, but for religious and social reasons.

Mainace

Riace bronze warrior.

Magna Graecia
The south of Italy and Sicily had so many colonies that the area was known as *Magna Graecia* (Great Greece). The natural harbours, rich farmland and closeness to Greece made them ideal spots to settle. Greek influence spread throughout Italy, and it was here that the Romans learnt of the Greek ways which they adopted to build their Empire.

Riace bronze warrior.

Etruria
No colonies were founded north of Naples in Italy, because of the Etruscans. However, Etruria (Tuscany) was rich in metals and there was a brisk trade between the two civilizations.

ITALY

● Aleria

Gold crown, from Taranto.

Metal coin, in the Greek style, from Naples.

● Naples

Taranto ●

● Selinus **SICILY** ● Rhegium

Carthage ●
(Phoenician city)

Gela ● ● Syracuse

NORTH AFRICA

Greek Colonies

The Greeks established overseas colonies from the 8th–5th centuries BC. They settled mainly along the northern shores of the Mediterranean and around the Black Sea, where rival civilizations such as the Phoenicians, Egyptians or Etruscans were not already in power. The first colonies probably served as trading stations where the Greeks could exchange their pottery and luxury goods for food and raw materials. Many settlements were positioned strategically so that the inhabitants could trade along routes and rivers leading to far-off civilizations, like the Celts in northern Europe and Mesopotamia in the Middle East. Other colonies, particularly in southern Italy and Sicily, were settled by farmers. Although the colonies were independent of their mother-cities in Greece, their inhabitants continued to live, farm, build cities and make pottery in the Greek style. Greek culture had an important and lasting influence in many of these areas. Through trade and other contact some elements of Greek culture even reached places where the Greeks themselves had never set foot.

In Sicily, many Greek temples have survived to the present day.

The Phoenicians
The Phoenicians, a trading people based in the Levant (modern Syria, Lebanon and Israel) were the Greeks' main rivals in the Mediterranean at this time. There was some exchange between the two; the Greek alphabet is based on the earlier Phoenician one, and many Greek (or Greek-influenced) artefacts have been found in ancient Phoenician cities.

Later settlements

Although the main period of colonization was from about BC 750-550, the Greeks continued to settle in other countries after that. They arrived in the Balkan islands of Dalmatia during the 4th century BC. They met with fierce resistance from the local Illyrian people and a series of wars ensued.

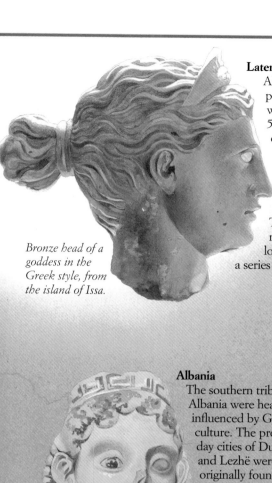

Bronze head of a goddess in the Greek style, from the island of Issa.

Trading colonies

Many of the Black Sea colonies were established for trade. The Greeks exchanged pottery and other luxury goods for grain, which they shipped back to the homeland. Greek influence in pottery and other crafts gradually spread great distances and mixed with local forms.

Greek-Scythian earring.

A gold statue of the Greek goddess Aphrodite, made by the Bactrian people in far-off central Asia.

Tanais

Panticapaeum

Albania

The southern tribes of Albania were heavily influenced by Greek culture. The present-day cities of Durrës and Lezhë were originally founded as Greek colonies.

Istrus

Black Sea jewellery

Some stunning examples of Greek jewellery have been found in Ancient Scythia, an area bordering the northern shores of the Black Sea. Archaeologists believe that they were made by Greek jewellers living in Scythia because while the craftsmen were clearly Greek, they had an excellent knowledge of life among the Scyth people.

Phasis

BLACK SEA

Sinope   Amisus

Trapezeus

Head of a sphinx, in the Corinthian style, dating from the 6th century BC.

cyra

Herakleia

Abdera   Byzantium

Consulting the oracle

As with all important decisions, an oracle was consulted before founding a colony. Many people gathered at popular oracles, such as Delphi. Besides consulting the oracle, colonialists also got up-to-date information about founding a colony.

Abydus

Preparing for departure

When a new colony was to be founded, the heads of the mother-city chose an official leader. He was responsible for the voyage, setting up new homes and distributing the land and other riches in the colony. The leader was honoured as the Founder, and was remembered and celebrated with more reverence than the mother-city itself.

A bowl decoration shows a man consulting the oracle of Apollo at Delphi.

GREECE

ANATOLIA   Phaselis

Al Mina

MEDITERRANEAN SEA

The black dots on the map show some of the larger or more important Greek colonies.

The city states in Anatolia (modern Turkey) were part of the Greek homelands.

The importance of agriculture

Many parts of Greece are arid with poor soils and farming is difficult at the best of times. As the population increased in the city-states more land was needed to grow food crops. When Greek farmers emigrated they found better farmland for themselves and relieved pressure on land at home.

Statue of the Greek god Poseidon, found in Israel.

PHOENICIA

Cyrene

A vase painting shows King Arkesilas of Cyrene over-seeing the weighing and storage of herbs grown in North Africa.

Colonies in the Middle East

The Phoenicians and Egyptians only allowed the Greeks to set up a few small trading colonies in this area. They were positioned strategically for access to important trade routes. For example, Al Mina, in Syria, was at the start of an overland route to Mesopotamia.

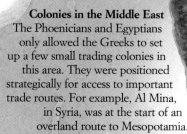

Greek Religion

The giant Atlas fought against the Olympians. In punishment, Zeus condemned him to carry the sky on his shoulders.

Demeter was a very ancient goddess. She is usually shown holding an ear of corn, sheaf of grain or basket of fruit and flowers.

Religion was an essential part of Greek life. It was not thought of as a separate action reserved for special days or occasions, but entered into every part of daily life. Important state decisions, such as whether to go to war or not, were only made after consulting one of the gods through an oracle. Private decisions, for example about whom to marry or trade with, were also made on the advice of a seer. Every official group of Greeks was a religious group, from the household, to the village, to the *polis* itself. All were dedicated to the worship of one or more gods; if, for example, your *polis* was dedicated, as Athens was, to the goddess Athena, then you were automatically a part of her cult and required to worship her.

Apollo was one of the most important gods. His main shrine was at Delphi.

The gods
There were many gods in the Greek pantheon, most of whom were Zeus' brothers, sisters or children. Zeus was called 'the father of gods and men'. Zeus' family was thought to live in a sprawling palace high on Mount Olympus. Its members were known as the Olympians. There was another group of gods, gathered around the figure of Hades, god of death. They were known as gods of the Underworld and were thought to live deep inside the Earth.

Demeter – goddess of agriculture
Demeter's name means 'grain mother' or 'mother earth'. She was worshipped throughout Greece as the goddess of agriculture. Festivals were held in her honour to celebrate the return of spring, and at harvest time in autumn.

Oracles, seers and omens
An oracle is a communication from a god in reply to a question (and also the place where the prophecy takes place). A stone tablet from Dodona, the oracle of Zeus, bears a typical question. 'Heracleidas asks the god whether he will have children from the wife he has now?' At Dodona, the god's reply was interpreted by priestesses from the rustling of leaves in the nearby trees. There were also wandering oracle-sellers with books of prophecies, and seers who foretold future events by looking at the entrails of animals and from the flight of birds.

A funeral procession, like the one shown below, was a solemn occasion with special rituals to be carried out by family and close friends.

Rites of passage
Many rituals had to do with the passing of an individual through the various stages of life. Private rites were celebrated at birth, marriage and death. A family ceremony was held five days after the birth of a child, to welcome it into the household. Death too was a private affair; the corpse was laid out by the women of the family and the funeral procession and burial were typically small. Public events were held when boys were prepared to become warriors, and girls to be mothers.

THE ACROPOLIS, IN CLASSICAL ATHENS.

There were many statues of Athena on the Acropolis. The peplos of the Panathenaia was offered to Athena Polis.

Contacting the gods

When people wanted to contact a god to ask a favour or receive help, they often sacrificed an animal to him or her. Many gods had favourite animals. Demeter liked pigs, Athena cows and Dionysus bulls. The animals were adorned with coloured ribbons and led to the altar, where a priest recited a prayer before slaughtering them.

The Panathenaia Festival procession.

The All-Athens Festival

The Panathenaia was held in June each year, on Athena's birthday. Once every four years it was especially lavish. A great procession (in which everybody took part, including foreigners and non-citizens) carried Athena's new *peplos* (woollen dress) across the city to her dwelling on the Acropolis. Cows were sacrificed, and a great feast followed. Everyone joined in to eat the meat of the sacrificial cows.

The huge golden Athena Parthenos (right) stood in the main temple, the Parthenon.

Festivals

Greek religion was not always solemn. The gods were thought to be pleased by festivals and many were held throughout the year. The Athenian calendar was so crowded with feast days that one ancient writer asked how it was possible to conduct business there! There were monthly festivals to celebrate divine birthdays and agricultural festivals, and days to remember the dead, as well as private rituals. The two largest festivals in Athens were the Panathenaia (All-Athens Festival) and the City Dionysia. During the Dionysia, dramatic and lyric poetry were performed in the theatre of Dionysus, near the Acropolis.

Gods and goddesses

Greek religion recognized a large number of female gods, many of whom were powerful, independent figures. This seems strange in a society that kept its women in strict seclusion and away from the main affairs of male life. Some historians think that the goddesses were part of Mediterranean and Eastern cults that existed before the Greeks arrived from the north, bringing their male gods with them.

Aphrodite was the goddess of love and beauty.

Delphi – the navel of the world

Apollo's oracle at Delphi was one of the oldest and most important. Because it was politically independent people came from all over the ancient world to consult it. For Zeus, it was 'the navel of the world', because when he sent two eagles from either end of the cosmos to find the centre of the Earth, they met at Delphi.

The gods and people

Unlike the gods of many modern religions, Greek divinities were often busy with their own affairs. They were not constantly watching over what people were doing on Earth. When they did have dealings with people, they were often nasty and selfish, rather than helpful to humans. The actions of the gods, their wars, love affairs and relationships with people, are all related in Greek mythology.

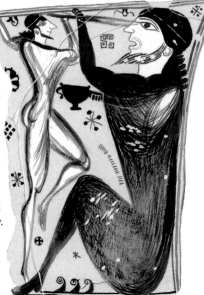

The human hero, Odysseus, is shown as he pokes the eye from a Cyclop's (one-eyed giant) head.

Main religious centres

The Greeks were polytheists, which means that they worshipped a number of different gods. The most important gods were worshipped all over the Greek world. Many had large sanctuaries dedicated to them in various parts of Greece. The map shows some of the more important sanctuaries.

Dodona *Zeus*

Ege *Poseidon*
Delphi *Apollo*
Corinth *Poseidon*
Mycenae *Hera*
Eleusis *Demeter*
Olympia *Zeus*
Athens *Athena*
Epidaurus *Asklepios*
Halicarnassus *Poseidon*
Sparta *Artemis, Hera*

Rhodes *Aphrodite*

The Greeks at War

Greek armies often employed paid soldiers, or mercenaries. This is an archer from Scythia.

The Greeks fought many wars over the centuries. Some were with outsiders, like the ones they fought against their powerful neighbour – the Persian Empire – from about 492–449 BC. Others were internal wars, like the Peloponnesian War (431–404 BC) between Athens and Sparta, which involved almost all the other city-states as well. Just a few decades later Alexander the Great conquered one of the largest empires the world had ever known. In archaic times wars were fought by kings and aristocrats mounted in chariots and combat was man-to-man. With the birth of the city-state, large armies and navies were formed. Foot soldiers, called hoplites, fought in phalanxes to overcome their enemy by sheer numbers. Many city-states built powerful navies; warships grew rapidly in size and in the numbers of men they carried. The mainstay of the Greek navies was the trireme, manned by 170 rowers. Early in the 4th century BC, the Athenian fleet boasted 400 triremes. Later, even larger warships were built. One of the largest, built by Ptolemy in the 3rd century BC, may have carried as many as 7,000 men.

Hoplites

Greek foot soldiers, called hoplites, wore heavy armour and carried a sword, a shield and a long thrusting spear. In battle, hoplites were massed together in phalanx formation. Eight ranks of hoplites one behind the other were able to force their way through enemy lines. This new way of fighting, based on the weight of many men together rather than the skilful fighting of a single soldier, was invented by the Greeks.

Relief carving, from 450 BC, of Ulysses as he stands unrecognized before his wife Penelope.

A painting on a Greek vase shows two phalanxes of hoplites as they go to battle. Note the fearsome faces painted on their shields and the musician playing the flute as he accompanies them into battle.

Bronze helmet from Corinth.

Heavy bronze breastplates protected the hoplites from the thrusts of the enemy's swords, spears and arrows.

A hero's welcome

Ulysses was the hero of Homer's long poem the *Iliad*. He was a wise king and a skilled warrior. After capturing the city of Troy, he wandered for nine years as he tried to get back to Ithaca and his wife Penelope. He was dressed as a beggar when he finally returned and his faithful old dog was the only one to recognize him.

The first warships

Early war galleys had fewer rowers aboard and were much slower than the trireme. Before the ram was invented, the oarsmen were also soldiers. When they reached the battleground they abandoned their oars and took up swords. Gradually the size of the boats and number of oarsmen increased. The penteconter was the basic unit in Greek fleets before the trireme. Penteconters were about 38 metres long. They were manned by 50 oarsmen. They had large heavy rams, often carved in the shape of a boar's head.

Greaves were worn to protect knees and shins.

The penteconter was a one-level galley. The oarsmen, sitting at deck level, were protected by leather covers.

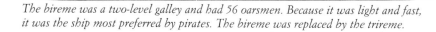

The bireme was a two-level galley and had 56 oarsmen. Because it was light and fast, it was the ship most preferred by pirates. The bireme was replaced by the trireme.

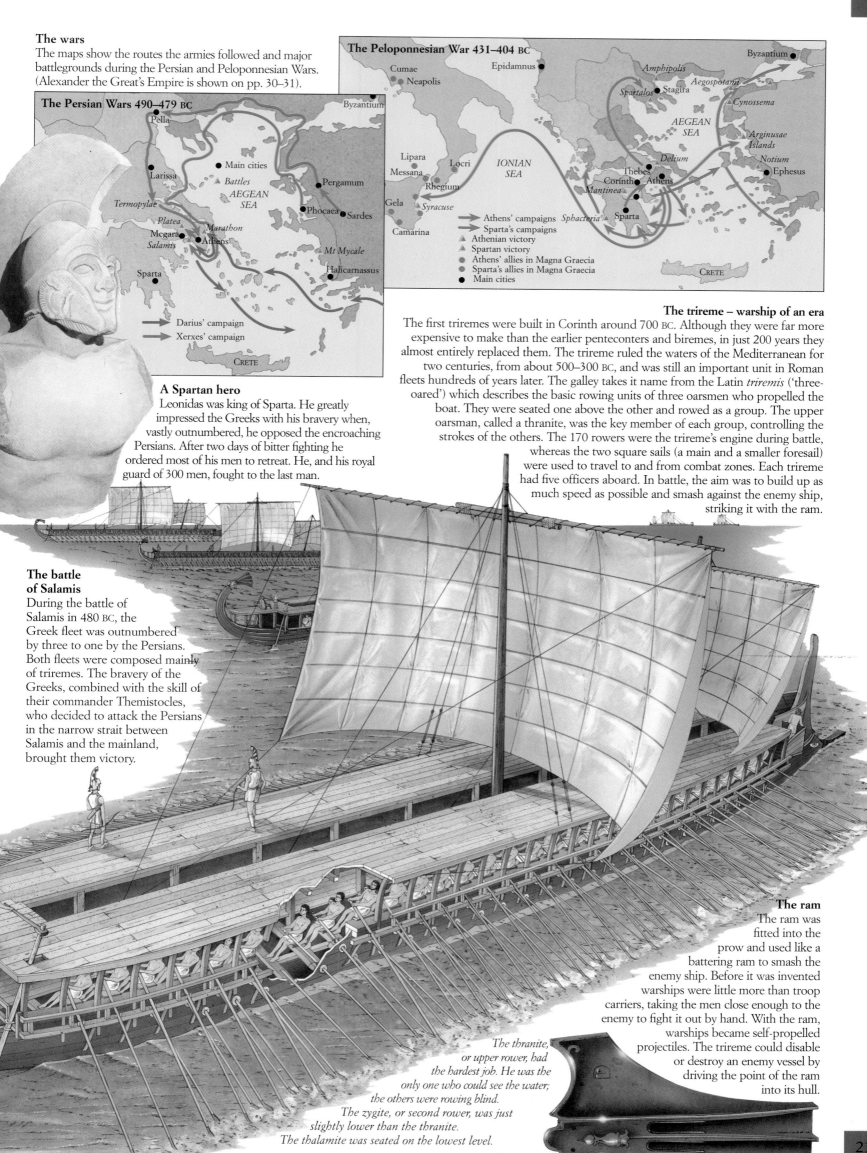

The wars
The maps show the routes the armies followed and major battlegrounds during the Persian and Peloponnesian Wars. (Alexander the Great's Empire is shown on pp. 30–31).

The Persian Wars 490–479 BC

- Pella
- Byzantium
- Larissa
- Main cities
- *Battles*
- *AEGEAN SEA*
- Pergamum
- *Termopylae*
- *Platea*
- *Marathon*
- Megara
- *Salamis*
- Athens
- Phocaea
- Sardes
- Sparta
- *Mt Mycale*
- Halicarnassus
- CRETE

→ Darius' campaign
→ Xerxes' campaign

The Peloponnesian War 431–404 BC

- Byzantium
- Cumae
- Epidamnus
- *Amphipolis*
- *Aegospotami*
- Neapolis
- *Spartalos* Stagira
- *Cynossema*
- *AEGEAN SEA*
- *Arginusae Islands*
- Lipara
- *Delium*
- Notium
- Messana
- Locri
- *IONIAN SEA*
- Thebes
- Ephesus
- Rhegium
- Corinth Athens
- Gela
- *Mantinea*
- *Syracuse*
- *Sphacteria* △ Sparta
- Camarina

→ Athens' campaigns
→ Sparta's campaigns
△ Athenian victory
△ Spartan victory
● Athens' allies in Magna Graecia
● Sparta's allies in Magna Graecia
● Main cities

CRETE

A Spartan hero
Leonidas was king of Sparta. He greatly impressed the Greeks with his bravery when, vastly outnumbered, he opposed the encroaching Persians. After two days of bitter fighting he ordered most of his men to retreat. He, and his royal guard of 300 men, fought to the last man.

The trireme – warship of an era
The first triremes were built in Corinth around 700 BC. Although they were far more expensive to make than the earlier penteconters and biremes, in just 200 years they almost entirely replaced them. The trireme ruled the waters of the Mediterranean for two centuries, from about 500–300 BC, and was still an important unit in Roman fleets hundreds of years later. The galley takes it name from the Latin *triremis* ('three-oared') which describes the basic rowing units of three oarsmen who propelled the boat. They were seated one above the other and rowed as a group. The upper oarsman, called a thranite, was the key member of each group, controlling the strokes of the others. The 170 rowers were the trireme's engine during battle, whereas the two square sails (a main and a smaller foresail) were used to travel to and from combat zones. Each trireme had five officers aboard. In battle, the aim was to build up as much speed as possible and smash against the enemy ship, striking it with the ram.

The battle of Salamis
During the battle of Salamis in 480 BC, the Greek fleet was outnumbered by three to one by the Persians. Both fleets were composed mainly of triremes. The bravery of the Greeks, combined with the skill of their commander Themistocles, who decided to attack the Persians in the narrow strait between Salamis and the mainland, brought them victory.

The ram
The ram was fitted into the prow and used like a battering ram to smash the enemy ship. Before it was invented warships were little more than troop carriers, taking the men close enough to the enemy to fight it out by hand. With the ram, warships became self-propelled projectiles. The trireme could disable or destroy an enemy vessel by driving the point of the ram into its hull.

The thranite, or upper rower, had the hardest job. He was the only one who could see the water; the others were rowing blind. The zygite, or second rower, was just slightly lower than the thranite. The thalamite was seated on the lowest level.

Hunting

Hunting was a popular sport among wealthy Greeks. Hares, deer and wild boars were common catches. Although hunters cooked and ate the animals they caught, it was a limited source of meat.

Inside of a cup showing a huntsman with his dog, a fox and a hare.

Fishing

Fishing was important to the Greek economy. Many towns and villages were located near the sea and the local people caught shellfish and other kinds of fish to eat and sell. As cities grew, fresh and pickled fish became important trading items.

Fisherman at work, from a vase painting.

A sleek pirate galley under full sail pursues a Greek merchantman. From a painting on a cup from Athens.

Agriculture and Trade

Greece is a mountainous country and only about a fifth of the land is suitable for farming. The climate is also unfavourable for agriculture – the long, hot summers with little rainfall are followed by cold winters. This meant not only that peasant farmers lived hard lives, but also that they were usually unable to produce more food than they needed themselves. As the population of Greece increased, more and more grain had to be imported to feed the people. Records show that the city government of Athens passed laws to keep grain prices steady, protect the sea routes along which grain was transported, and to force merchants to bring their cargoes to the city port at Piraeus. The cities of mainland Greece imported huge quantities of cereals, wine, olive oil, salt-fish and *garum* (fish sauce used to flavour dishes) from their colonies and neighbouring countries, such as Egypt. They even went as far afield as southern Russia, where rich soils produced far more food than the local population consumed. The Greeks paid for their imports by exporting exquisitely painted pottery, jewellery and other craftwork, as well as wine and oil produced in Asia Minor and the colonies. Almost all trading was done by sea, and sturdy vessels, called merchantmen, were built to haul cargoes far and wide.

Merchantmen

Freighters were powered by sail and oar. Liquid cargo, such as oil and wine, was carried in large clay containers, called amphorae. Since a standard Greek term for a freighter was a 'ten-thousander', referring to the number of amphorae or sacks of grain that could be loaded aboard, some of them were obviously very large.

Women's contribution to the economy

Greek women, rich and poor, were responsible for spinning and weaving. Every kind of fabric object, from pillows and blankets to winter cloaks, was produced in the home. Imported cloth and silk were rare luxuries.

Pirates

The seas were full of vessels carrying valuable cargoes, and piracy was common. To ward off attack traders sometimes travelled in convoys of up to 250 vessels, escorted by warships. They were most vulnerable in narrow straits like the one separating the Black Sea from the Mediterranean.

A painted cup in the form of a donkey's head. Greek potters were very skilful.

Merchants

Small traders operated from workshops near the *agora*. Larger merchants were usually based near a port where they kept ships and controlled imports and exports. Some merchants became very rich. As trade expanded bankers appeared who made loans, often charging very high interest rates.

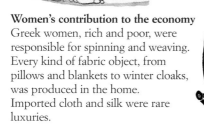

Weighing goods for sale and export.

Trade

The map shows the most frequently traded goods.

pottery

wool

salt-fish

fabrics

minerals

wine

glass

marble

cereals

olive oil

timber

slaves

Coin with a turtle, from the Greek island of Aegina.

ATLANTIC OCEAN

R. Rhine

R. Danube

BLACK SEA

IBERIA

ITALY

ANATOLIA

TYRRHENIAN SEA

AEGEAN SEA

• Athens

IONIAN SEA

MEDITERRANEAN SEA

AFRICA

R. Nile

This silver coin with an ear of barley shows how important cereals were.

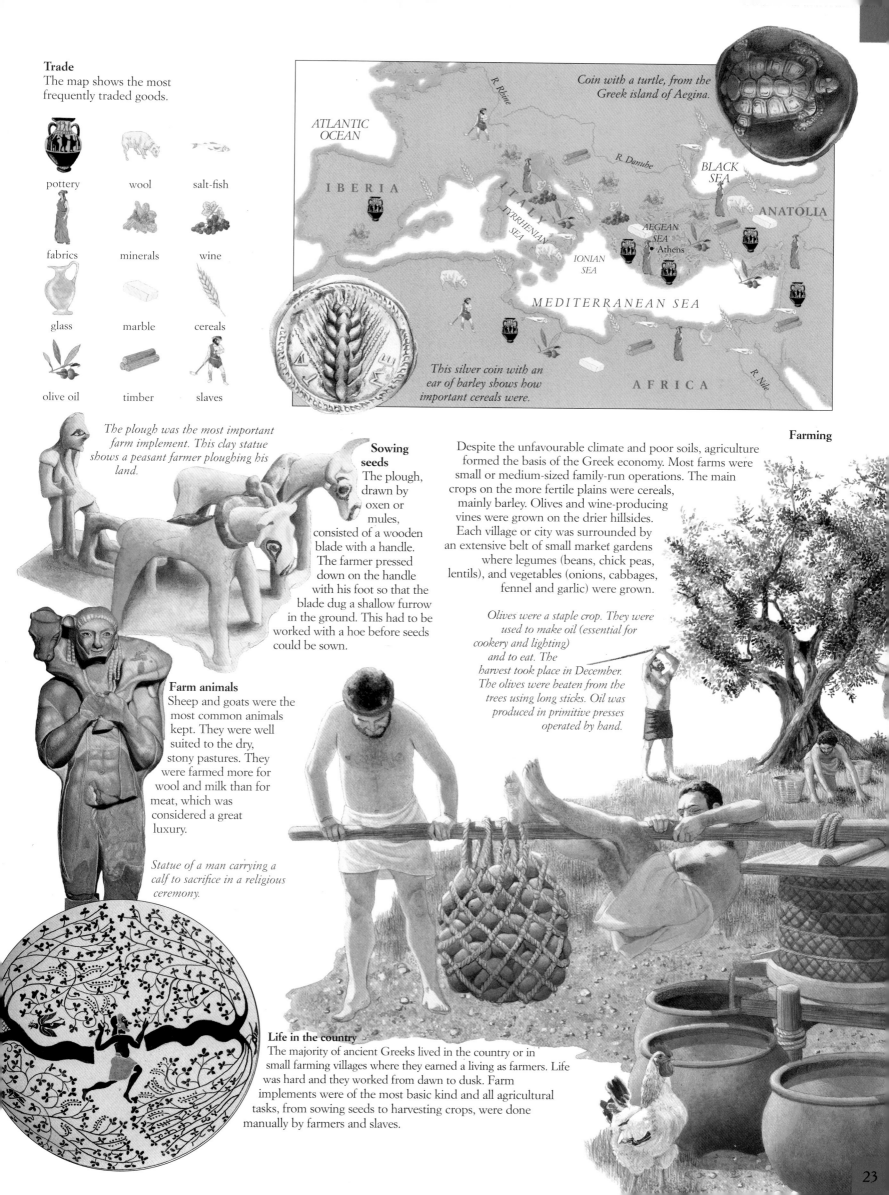

The plough was the most important farm implement. This clay statue shows a peasant farmer ploughing his land.

Sowing seeds

The plough, drawn by oxen or mules, consisted of a wooden blade with a handle. The farmer pressed down on the handle with his foot so that the blade dug a shallow furrow in the ground. This had to be worked with a hoe before seeds could be sown.

Farming

Despite the unfavourable climate and poor soils, agriculture formed the basis of the Greek economy. Most farms were small or medium-sized family-run operations. The main crops on the more fertile plains were cereals, mainly barley. Olives and wine-producing vines were grown on the drier hillsides. Each village or city was surrounded by an extensive belt of small market gardens where legumes (beans, chick peas, lentils), and vegetables (onions, cabbages, fennel and garlic) were grown.

Olives were a staple crop. They were used to make oil (essential for cookery and lighting) and to eat. The harvest took place in December. The olives were beaten from the trees using long sticks. Oil was produced in primitive presses operated by hand.

Farm animals

Sheep and goats were the most common animals kept. They were well suited to the dry, stony pastures. They were farmed more for wool and milk than for meat, which was considered a great luxury.

Statue of a man carrying a calf to sacrifice in a religious ceremony.

Life in the country

The majority of ancient Greeks lived in the country or in small farming villages where they earned a living as farmers. Life was hard and they worked from dawn to dusk. Farm implements were of the most basic kind and all agricultural tasks, from sowing seeds to harvesting crops, were done manually by farmers and slaves.

Greek Theatre

In the beginning Greek theatre was closely tied to religious ceremonies. Over the centuries, plays began to deal with subjects from Homer's poetry or with everyday political or social themes and theatre gradually became an art, separate from religion. There were two main types of drama – Tragedy and Comedy. Tragedy dealt with important people and events and each play, based on legend or history, delivered some moral, religious or political message to the spectators. Comedy plays were witty, grotesque, and often bawdy and vulgar. Later comic plays became satires of modern city life. The first dramatic festival was held in Athens in 534 BC at the great spring festival, the City Dionysia. After that each Dionysia included four consecutive days of theatre when spectators sat from dawn till dusk comparing the works of specially chosen playwrights. Unfortunately, out of the enormous number of plays written, only thirty-five tragedies (by Aeschylus, Sophocles and Euripides) and a few comedies (mainly by Aristophanes) have survived. They are still performed regularly in many parts of the world.

Tragic mask from the 3rd century BC.

Large bronze votive mask with horrified eyes. It is a copy of a mask that a tragic actor would have worn in the 5th century.

Mask worn by an actor during a comedy.

Music

Theatrical pieces were accompanied by music and singing. Flutes, drums, lyre, pipes and cymbals were some of the most common instruments used.

Masks

Actors and members of the chorus all wore masks covering their faces and heads during the entire performance.

Relief showing the playwright Menander seated in a workshop supervising the making of masks for one of his comedies.

This 2nd century BC mosaic of a tragic mask shows how expressive masks could be.

The theatre

Greek plays were performed in open-air theatres. The theatres were semicircular, with steep-sided stone seating for the audience. The seating was usually built into a hillside. The chorus appeared in the orchestra at ground level and the actors on the raised stage above it. A large theatre could hold up to 12,000 spectators. Acoustics in many theatres were perfect and even those seated in the top rows could hear every word the actors spoke.

Each theatre had one or more fine marble seats in the front row near the stage where an important citizen or visitor could be seated.

Theatre with a tunnel near the stage. Actors could 'disappear' from the scene.

Special effects

Greek theatre made use of many special effects, including hoists to lift actors off the stage, revolving scenes, hidden tunnels, and rolling stones under the spectators' seats to imitate the sound of thunder.

Theatre with a hoist so that actors could 'fly' away or appear or disappear as if by magic.

The actors

There were usually only three actors in each play. They were all men. Since most plays had many characters, each actor had to play several roles, both male and female. Each time they changed character they would change their masks so that the audience could see who they were representing.

Tragedies and comedies

Most tragedies were inspired by the works of Homer. They were epic dramas about serious themes in human life. Comedies were lighter works, often dealing with contemporary themes. They were often very critical of government or politicians, or certain classes of people in society in a biting, but lighthearted way.

The chorus

From the 5th century onwards a group of people, called the chorus, worked out front in the orchestra during each performance. The chorus had fifteen members for tragedies, twenty-four for comedies, and twelve for satyric plays. The chorus usually entered after the prologue. They sang, danced, acted and even exchanged comments with the actors on the stage above them during the performance.

Vase painting showing three members of the chorus dressed as horses with three others riding them.

This vase painting shows an actor playing the part of the god Zeus as he tries to climb up to a woman's window with a ladder. Many plays were based on incidents from Greek mythology.

The most famous play

Oedipus the King, by Sophocles, is the most famous Greek tragedy. It tells the story of King Oedipus who became ruler of Thebes by correctly answering a sphinx's riddle. Without knowing, Oedipus then kills his own father and marries his mother. When he finds out what he has done he sticks needles into his eyes, blinding himself.

Oedipus answering the sphinx's riddle.

The location of theatres

The map shows the location of some of the larger or more important theatres in ancient Greece. Many theatres were later used by the Romans. Some are still in use today.

Costume

The actors' costumes helped explain who they were playing. Some characters had special, recognizable costumes. For example, we know that the man on the right is acting the part of Herakles, because he is carrying a club and wearing a lion's skin – two symbols of this hero.

This scene from a vase painting shows the key episode in the play Agamemnon, *by Aeschylus. It depicts the Greek king Agamemnon as he is murdered on his return home after the Trojan War.*

Aeschylus

Aeschylus was the first of the great Athenian dramatists. He lived from about 525–455 BC. He was called the 'Father of Greek Tragedy'.

Scene from Aeschylus' play Eumenides. *It shows Apollo throwing the Furies out of the temple.*

Science and Literature

Greek poets, philosophers, scientists and mathematicians made a profound and lasting contribution to the formation of Western culture. The works of poets, such as Homer and Sappho, have been studied and read as classics for over 2,000 years. Many of the ideas first advanced by Greek philosophers are still being discussed. Many scientific and mathematical theories from ancient Greece are still in use. Greek philosophers and scientists were the first Europeans to base their knowledge on direct observation of the world around them, rather than on mythological or supernatural beliefs. They believed that people could know and explain everything in the world through observation and reasoning.

Ancient bust of a man, said to be Homer.

Homer
The author of the two greatest Greek epic poems – the *Iliad* and the *Odyssey* – is thought to have lived in the 9th or 8th century BC. Scholars know almost nothing about Homer's life. His works were very important for the ancient Greeks who saw them as symbols of Greek unity. They have greatly influenced Western literature for almost 3,000 years. Both epics have been translated into all the modern European languages many times.

Aspasia

Although most women were never taught to read and write, a few did become important intellectuals. These women generally lived outside the respectable upper classes. Aspasia, the most famous woman in 5th-century Athens, was the companion of the statesman Pericles. She was famous for her intelligence and political astuteness.

Herodotus – the 'Father of history'
Herodotus lived in the 5th century BC. He is famous as the author of the first great book of history, on the Graeco-Persian Wars. Herodotus travelled widely; he was very interested in the customs and history of the Greeks and their enemies, the Persians. He was tolerant and open-minded with no bias for his fellow countrymen. His *History* remains the leading source of information for Greek history between 550–479 BC.

Wall-painting of a woman with wooden writing tablets and stylus from Pompeii in southern Italy, 1st century AD. The very refined style shows strong Greek influence.

Astronomy
A Greek scientist, Aristarchus of Samos (c. 310–230 BC), was the first to discover that the earth rotates once every 24 hours and that, together with the other planets in our solar system, it revolves around the sun. His theory was dismissed for almost seventeen centuries, until Copernicus proved him correct. Up until then the views of another Greek astronomer, Hipparchus (2nd century BC), held sway. He believed that the earth lay at the centre of the universe and that the sun and planets revolved around it. Even so, Hipparchus made many important discoveries, including the precession of the equinoxes and the length of a year.

Hippocrates – the 'Father of medicine'
The books in the *Hippocratic Collection* (5th century BC – probably written by one man, called Hippocrates), mark the stage where disease came to be seen as a natural phenomenon, rather than being caused by the gods or other supernatural forces. From this time onwards doctors began to look for physical causes and cures for sickness. The Hippocratic oath, an ethical code of conduct for doctors, has guided the practise of Western medicine for more than 2,000 years.

The Trojan War, the legendary conflict between the Greeks and the people of Troy celebrated in the works of Homer, may have taken place in the 13th–12th centuries BC. The Greeks defeated the Trojans by introducing a large wooden horse full of soldiers into Troy. The scene above comes from a pot dated about 675 BC.

Philosophical discussion
Greek men gathered together not only for relaxation and drinking parties, but also to discuss important political and philosophical ideas. Many of the works of the ancient Greek philosophers are written in the form of dialogues. In these books an idea is developed in the form of a conversation between a number of men.

Sappho
The Greek poet Sappho lived from about 610–580 BC on the island of Lesbos, near modern Turkey. Her poems are intensely personal, dealing mainly with her friendships and feuds with other women. Although much of her poetry has been lost, we know about it secondhand from scholars who studied it in the centuries after her death.

Aristarchus of Samos correctly maintained that the earth revolves around the sun over 2,200 years ago.

Sun

Earth

Moon

$A^2 + B^2 = C^2$
The Greeks achieved some brilliant successes in geometry. Pythagoras' theory concerning right angle triangles is still taught to children throughout the world.

A

C

B

Model of Hero of Alexandria's aeolipile, or the first steam-powered engine. Designed in the 1st century AD, it is a forerunner of the jet engine.

The great three – Socrates, Plato and Aristotle

Socrates (470–399 BC) was the first of the great trio of ancient Greek philosophers. He was a good man, believing that no one should ever do wrong or take part, even indirectly, in wrongdoing. He also thought that if people really knew what was right and good they could never do wrong. Plato (428–348 BC) was a disciple of Socrates. He travelled widely after Socrates' death before founding the Academy for philosophy in Athens. Plato is still considered one of the greatest philosophical writers. Aristotle (384–322 BC) was both a philosopher and a scientist. He studied at the Academy for twenty years until Plato died. Much later Aristotle founded the Lyceum, an important centre for study and research into every branch of knowledge.

Technology

Many of the scientific discoveries were used to invent new and wonderful machines. Many were planned but never built. Those that were built were more often used for entertainment than for practical purposes. Rudimentary steam engines, automatic fountains and revolving ceilings are examples of just some of the inventions made.

Mathematics

Although some of the theories they developed were invented by earlier civilizations, such as the Babylonians and Egyptians, the ancient Greeks are sometimes called the inventors of mathematics because they were the first to make it a theoretical discipline. This means that all mathematical statements had to be general and had to be confirmed by proof. The work of Greek mathematicians such as Pythagoras, Euclid, Archimedes and Apollonius (among others) lies at the basis of modern mathematics.

Bust of Socrates.

Philosophy

The word philosophy means 'love of wisdom'. Thales of Miletus, who lived in the 6th century BC, is considered the earliest Greek philosopher because he was the first to give a natural explanation of the origin of the world, rather than a mythological one. He was followed by many serious thinkers whose aim was to explain the world on the basis of what they could observe. Many of the most fundamental problems of Western philosophy were first discovered and discussed by these men.

Greek philosophers debating in the shade of an olive tree.

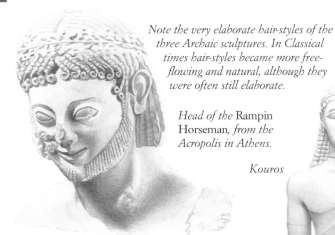

Note the very elaborate hair-styles of the three Archaic sculptures. In Classical times hair-styles became more free-flowing and natural, although they were often still elaborate.

Head of the Rampin Horseman, *from the Acropolis in Athens.*

Kouros

Kore

Traces of colour remain on the Kore *(left) from the Acropolis in Athens. Her hair and lips were painted red, her eyelashes and eyebrows black and the pattern on her dress green.*

Archaic sculpture 660–480 BC

Many of the Archaic sculptures that have survived are large statues or reliefs of *kouroi* (young men) or *korai* (young women). These early works are much less realistic than Classical statues. They have stylized facial expressions and many have a strange smile playing about their lips. The rigidity gradually disappeared and by 480 BC the statues began to take on the realistic, if idealized style of the Classical period.

Black-figure painting from an amphora *(jar), by the Athenian artist Exekias. It shows Achilles and Ajax playing a board game.*

The development of vase painting

The earliest vases (10th–9th centuries BC) have abstract decorations. By the 8th century BC, during the Geometric period, both abstract patterns and figures are used. Figures gradually came to predominate in the black-figure works from the 7th century BC onwards. Some of the most beautiful vases ever made came from Athens. The more realistic red-figure technique was invented there about 530 BC. Vase painting was an important art form all over the Greek world. The shape of the vase was less important than the way it was decorated. New and lively schools grew up in the Greek colonies, particularly in southern Italy and Sicily. By Hellenistic times (330 BC) the art of vase painting had almost died out.

Vase from the Geometric period. Note the figures near the neck of the jug.

Classical sculpture 480–330 BC

Classical sculpture represents a complete break with earlier traditions. For the first time in the history of Western art, artists showed that they had a complete and detailed understanding of the human body, of how it looks in action and in repose. It was the first time that people had shown the knowledge, and the desire, to represent humans, gods and the world around them with such realism.

Towards the more expressive Hellenistic period

Towards the end of the Classical period some great sculptors brought more life and expression back to the art. Praxiteles, Scopas and Lysippus all worked during the 4th century BC. They combined the technical know-how of earlier artists with increased ability and desire to show human emotions.

Wall painting, engraving and other arts

Painting on walls or panels was a popular and highly valued art in Classical times, even more so than vase painting. Unfortunately, very few paintings have survived. Engraving was another popular art; some striking pieces of jewellery, coins and finely decorated objects have been found. Records also show that beautiful cloths were woven and dyed, although almost nothing remains of these.

The city of Athens was a busy centre for crafts of all types. The workshops were located around the agora; *some quarters even took their names from the craftspeople who worked there. Pottery was important and production included fine decorative vases and everyday household objects. Leatherworkers produced bags, sandals and other objects of daily use.*

Better than nature

Classical sculptors not only copied nature, they tried to improve on it. Human anatomy is made perfect in statues of the period. The stunningly beautiful statues can sometimes seem cold or expressionless to modern viewers.

This 2nd-century BC marble statue from Melos, called the Venus de Milo, *shows the Greek goddess of love, Aphrodite. The High Classical perfection visible in, for example, the* Riace Bronzes (see p. 16) *has given way here to a more sensual portrayal.*

Red-figure vase showing craftsmen casting a bronze statue of a warrior.

Doric capital

Ionic capital

The Doric order
The Doric is the simplest of the Greek orders. The slightly tapered column is topped by a plain capital.

The Ionic order
The Ionic column has scrolls (called volutes) on the capital.

Corinthian capital

The Corinthian order
The Corinthian is the most ornate order. The capital has rich acanthus-leaf decorations.

This relief statue from the Parthenon frieze shows a centaur (half man, half horse) struggling with a man.

Warrior from the Parthenon frieze.

Horse head form the northeast corner of the Parthenon.

Sculpture on the Parthenon
The Parthenon temple was decorated with a continuous sculpted frieze showing scenes from the annual All-Athens Festival. Other magnificent pieces showed battle scenes.

Roman copy of a bronze head of a poet or philosopher.

Architecture
For a long time Greek architects were employed almost exclusively to design cult buildings (places of worship). They invented three different 'orders' of architecture – the Doric, Ionic and Corinthian. Each had a different style of column supporting the upper section of the temple. Until recently these three orders formed the basis of Western architecture. Magnificent temples of stone and marble were built throughout Greece and its colonies. After about 400 BC, architects began designing public buildings, like the *colonnade stoa* building in the *agora* in Athens.

The buildings on the Acropolis in Athens are among the most impressive works of architecture from the Classical period. The whole complex is shown on p. 6. The Erechtheum was a temple dedicated to different cults. Its Caryatid porch (shown here) makes use of figures of women in place of columns.

Sculpture in the Hellenistic world 330–100 BC
Sculpture in this period was very expressive. Emotions, such as triumph, fury and despair, are recreated in marble and bronze by exaggerating human anatomy and distorting features.

Greek Art and Craft

For the ancient Greeks art and craft were the same. They had no separate word for art in the way we use it. They spoke of *techne*, which is much closer to our word craft. They had no museums to display the many works they created, which were designed with more practical uses in mind. A beautiful statue was made and dedicated to a god or goddess, or used to commemorate an important historical event. Vases were produced and painted for export, or for local use as signs of wealth or to mark tombs. The astonishing temples that still dot the landscape of the Mediterranean region were built in honour of the gods. An important thing to remember when viewing ancient art today is that when they were created all sculptures and architecture were brightly coloured and very different from the austere white marble or sandstone we now see. Nevertheless, much ancient art has survived to the present day and it is one of the major sources through which we can learn about and admire the Greek world.

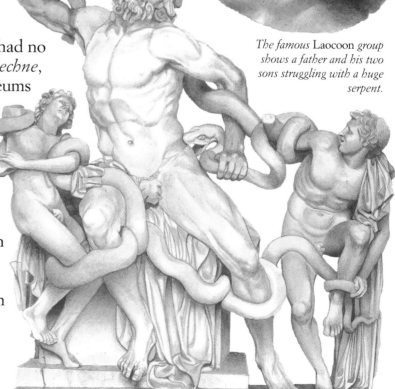
The famous Laocoon *group shows a father and his two sons struggling with a huge serpent.*

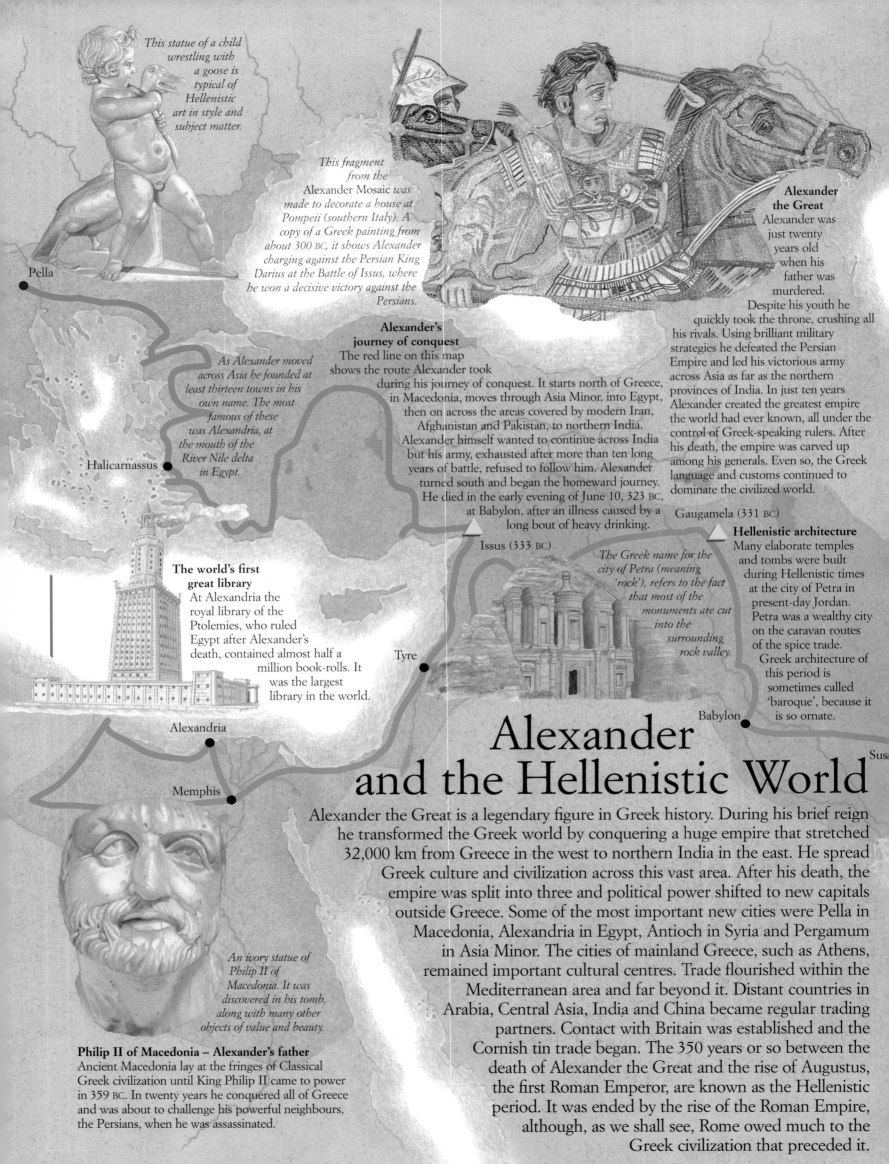

This statue of a child wrestling with a goose is typical of Hellenistic art in style and subject matter.

Pella

This fragment from the Alexander Mosaic was made to decorate a house at Pompeii (southern Italy). A copy of a Greek painting from about 300 BC, it shows Alexander charging against the Persian King Darius at the Battle of Issus, where he won a decisive victory against the Persians.

Alexander the Great
Alexander was just twenty years old when his father was murdered. Despite his youth he quickly took the throne, crushing all his rivals. Using brilliant military strategies he defeated the Persian Empire and led his victorious army across Asia as far as the northern provinces of India. In just ten years Alexander created the greatest empire the world had ever known, all under the control of Greek-speaking rulers. After his death, the empire was carved up among his generals. Even so, the Greek language and customs continued to dominate the civilized world.

As Alexander moved across Asia he founded at least thirteen towns in his own name. The most famous of these was Alexandria, at the mouth of the River Nile delta in Egypt.

Halicarnassus

Alexander's journey of conquest
The red line on this map shows the route Alexander took during his journey of conquest. It starts north of Greece, in Macedonia, moves through Asia Minor, into Egypt, then on across the areas covered by modern Iran, Afghanistan and Pakistan, to northern India. Alexander himself wanted to continue across India but his army, exhausted after more than ten long years of battle, refused to follow him. Alexander turned south and began the homeward journey. He died in the early evening of June 10, 323 BC, at Babylon, after an illness caused by a long bout of heavy drinking.

Gaugamela (331 BC)

Hellenistic architecture
Many elaborate temples and tombs were built during Hellenistic times at the city of Petra in present-day Jordan. Petra was a wealthy city on the caravan routes of the spice trade.
Greek architecture of this period is sometimes called 'baroque', because it is so ornate.

Issus (333 BC)

The Greek name for the city of Petra (meaning 'rock'), refers to the fact that most of the monuments are cut into the surrounding rock valley.

The world's first great library
At Alexandria the royal library of the Ptolemies, who ruled Egypt after Alexander's death, contained almost half a million book-rolls. It was the largest library in the world.

Tyre

Alexandria

Babylon

Sus

Memphis

An ivory statue of Philip II of Macedonia. It was discovered in his tomb, along with many other objects of value and beauty.

Philip II of Macedonia – Alexander's father
Ancient Macedonia lay at the fringes of Classical Greek civilization until King Philip II came to power in 359 BC. In twenty years he conquered all of Greece and was about to challenge his powerful neighbours, the Persians, when he was assassinated.

Alexander and the Hellenistic World

Alexander the Great is a legendary figure in Greek history. During his brief reign he transformed the Greek world by conquering a huge empire that stretched 32,000 km from Greece in the west to northern India in the east. He spread Greek culture and civilization across this vast area. After his death, the empire was split into three and political power shifted to new capitals outside Greece. Some of the most important new cities were Pella in Macedonia, Alexandria in Egypt, Antioch in Syria and Pergamum in Asia Minor. The cities of mainland Greece, such as Athens, remained important cultural centres. Trade flourished within the Mediterranean area and far beyond it. Distant countries in Arabia, Central Asia, India and China became regular trading partners. Contact with Britain was established and the Cornish tin trade began. The 350 years or so between the death of Alexander the Great and the rise of Augustus, the first Roman Emperor, are known as the Hellenistic period. It was ended by the rise of the Roman Empire, although, as we shall see, Rome owed much to the Greek civilization that preceded it.

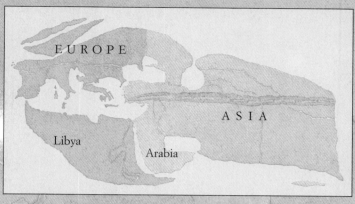

EUROPE

ASIA

Libya

Arabia

The Tazza Farnese is a famous piece of cameo art from Hellenistic times. It decorates the bottom of a cup. Just 20 cm in diameter, the interior of the cup (shown here) has a beautiful scene celebrating the fertility of the River Nile. The outside shows a mask of Medusa.

Hellenistic art

Some of the most beautiful examples of Greek sculpture date from the Hellenistic period. The famous artist Lysippus was Alexander's favourite sculptor. He created dramatic works of art that expressed a yearning for unattainable things. Many sculptures were very expressive and dramatic, but scenes of everyday life were also common.

Alexander broadens horizons

Greek maps of the world during the Classical period show Europe occupying a large space. After Alexander, Hellenistic maps, like the one below, showed Europe as a smaller corner of a much vaster world, in which Asia took up at least half the space.

This statue, called the Nike of Samothrace, shows the winged Greek goddess of victory alighting on the prow of a ship. With the wind whipping her garments, she is the embodiment of triumph. It was sculpted in 203 BC to commemorate a sea battle.

Alexander's leadership

Part of the myth of Alexander derives from the fact that he led his troops into battle himself, rather than watching from the sidelines. But Alexander was more than just a great soldier and military strategist, he was also an astute politician. He married many times during his journey, always choosing women from the local ruling family. Where he didn't marry, he often kept the ruling group in power, but under his control.

Alexandria Eschate

Alexander with his favourite horse, called Bucephalus.

Susia

Bactra

Alexander becomes a god

In the year leading up to his death, Alexander showed signs of strain and emotional instability. He often compared himself to the gods Herakles or Dionysus and requested that the Greek cities confer upon him the status of a god. Some cities did so, albeit ironically. The Spartans wrote 'If Alexander wishes to be a god, let him be a god.'

Bucephala (326 BC)

Alexandria

Coin showing Alexander fighting against the elephants in the army of King Porus in northern India.

Scholarship and learning

The period from about 300 to 150 BC was highly creative. Great writers and scholars met at rich courts financed by wealthy kings. Poetry, drama, history, philosophy and all the other various sciences and arts flourished under royal patronage. Greek was the language of all scholarship and the Classical authors were much studied.

The Persians

The mighty kings of Persia ruled over an Empire that encompassed most of the Near East for some 200 years. During that time they often clashed with the Greeks, although neither achieved longlasting victory until Alexander the Great defeated King Darius III at the Battle of Gaugamela in 331 BC. Before its downfall the Persian Empire was well organized. The land was divided into satrapies (provinces), well connected by good roads. The ancient Persians were skilled soldiers and craftspeople.

This gold statue of a winged ibex shows how skilled the Persians were at metalworking.

Zoroaster

The Persians worshipped a supreme god called Ahura Mazda. The prophet who taught them of this god was called Zoroaster; the religion they followed was named Zoroastrianism. It is still practised today in some parts of the world.

Persepolis

Alexandria

Pattala

Alexander left Greece on his journey into Asia with 40,000 foot soldiers and 6,000 cavalry. The Macedonian phalanx, armed with long spears, formed the core of the infantry.

Science and technology

Medicine, astronomy and mathematics were the three great areas of scientific scholarship in Hellenistic times.

Technological inventions included this water pump, called the Archimedes' screw, used to extract flood water from mines, for irrigation and for draining swampy land.

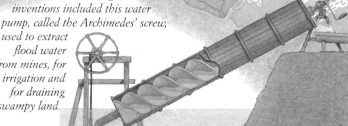

31

Sport in the Greek World

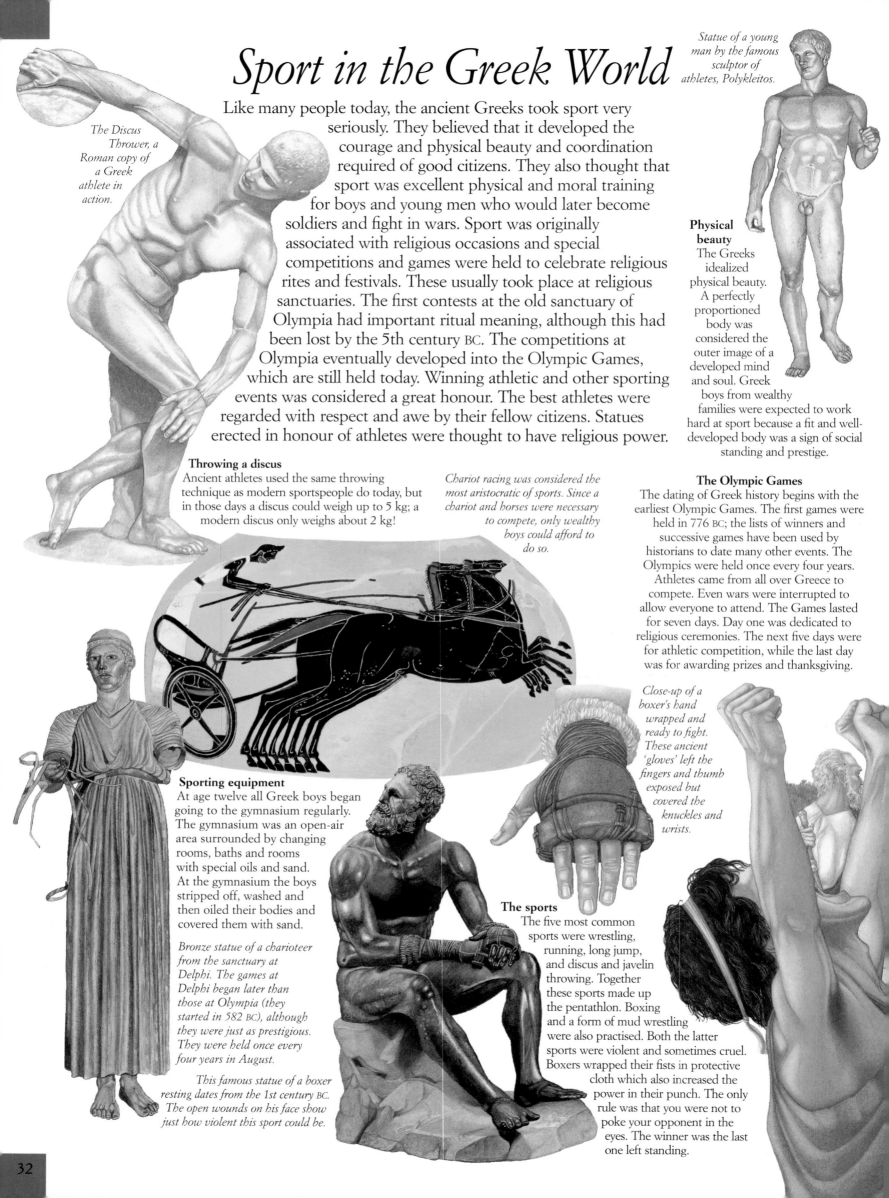

The Discus Thrower, a Roman copy of a Greek athlete in action.

Statue of a young man by the famous sculptor of athletes, Polykleitos.

Like many people today, the ancient Greeks took sport very seriously. They believed that it developed the courage and physical beauty and coordination required of good citizens. They also thought that sport was excellent physical and moral training for boys and young men who would later become soldiers and fight in wars. Sport was originally associated with religious occasions and special competitions and games were held to celebrate religious rites and festivals. These usually took place at religious sanctuaries. The first contests at the old sanctuary of Olympia had important ritual meaning, although this had been lost by the 5th century BC. The competitions at Olympia eventually developed into the Olympic Games, which are still held today. Winning athletic and other sporting events was considered a great honour. The best athletes were regarded with respect and awe by their fellow citizens. Statues erected in honour of athletes were thought to have religious power.

Physical beauty
The Greeks idealized physical beauty. A perfectly proportioned body was considered the outer image of a developed mind and soul. Greek boys from wealthy families were expected to work hard at sport because a fit and well-developed body was a sign of social standing and prestige.

Throwing a discus
Ancient athletes used the same throwing technique as modern sportspeople do today, but in those days a discus could weigh up to 5 kg; a modern discus only weighs about 2 kg!

Chariot racing was considered the most aristocratic of sports. Since a chariot and horses were necessary to compete, only wealthy boys could afford to do so.

The Olympic Games
The dating of Greek history begins with the earliest Olympic Games. The first games were held in 776 BC; the lists of winners and successive games have been used by historians to date many other events. The Olympics were held once every four years. Athletes came from all over Greece to compete. Even wars were interrupted to allow everyone to attend. The Games lasted for seven days. Day one was dedicated to religious ceremonies. The next five days were for athletic competition, while the last day was for awarding prizes and thanksgiving.

Sporting equipment
At age twelve all Greek boys began going to the gymnasium regularly. The gymnasium was an open-air area surrounded by changing rooms, baths and rooms with special oils and sand. At the gymnasium the boys stripped off, washed and then oiled their bodies and covered them with sand.

Bronze statue of a charioteer from the sanctuary at Delphi. The games at Delphi began later than those at Olympia (they started in 582 BC), although they were just as prestigious. They were held once every four years in August.

This famous statue of a boxer resting dates from the 1st century BC. The open wounds on his face show just how violent this sport could be.

Close-up of a boxer's hand wrapped and ready to fight. These ancient 'gloves' left the fingers and thumb exposed but covered the knuckles and wrists.

The sports
The five most common sports were wrestling, running, long jump, and discus and javelin throwing. Together these sports made up the pentathlon. Boxing and a form of mud wrestling were also practised. Both the latter sports were violent and sometimes cruel. Boxers wrapped their fists in protective cloth which also increased the power in their punch. The only rule was that you were not to poke your opponent in the eyes. The winner was the last one left standing.

Vase painting showing athletes during a running race. The athletes moved using alternate legs and arms together for balance and speed.

Close-up of the scraper.

Painting on a vase fragment. It shows spectators shouting and cheering during a chariot race just as they do today at a modern sporting event.

The marathon

As the years passed more and more events were added to the Olympic Games. The marathon was introduced in 490 BC after the Greeks won a decisive battle against the Persians at the city of Marathon. A Greek soldier, eager to let the Athenians know of their victory, ran the 42.195 km to Athens. He was so exhausted when he arrived that he died before being able to complete his triumphant message. The marathon was invented in his honour. Modern marathons are still run over exactly the same distance.

After the event

The athletes used a special instrument to scrape the sweat, oil and sand from their bodies after a sporting event. This famous statue by Lysippus shows an athlete scraping himself.

Greeks played a ball game (left) using curved sticks. It looks very similar to modern hockey. Two youths (right) begin a wrestling match. Wrestling was a fairly civilized sport in comparison with boxing and all-in fighting where athletes sometimes killed each other during the event.

Sequence showing the various phases of a long jump. Note the way the weights are used to balance the jump.

The weights were made of stone or metal and many, like this pair, have survived.

Long jump

Greek athletes carried weights in their hands during the long jump. The weights were very carefully shaped and were important in balancing the jump.

Women and sport

As in most other sectors of public life, women were excluded from sporting events. Many historians think that they were not even allowed to attend the various games as spectators. However, in some sanctuaries special athletic events were held for young women. Some historians think that young Spartan women competed regularly in athletic competitions.

Reconstruction of a women's sporting event in Sparta. The athletes wore short tunics. Some ancient writers were outraged because they thought they were not suitably modest.

The Origins of Rome

Before the Romans conquered the Italian peninsula it was inhabited by a variety of peoples of different origin, language, traditions and stage of development. The Etruscans were the most powerful and developed civilization (see pp. 36–37) and the neighbouring Greeks were influential, particularly after they established colonies in the south. The Latins, the people who would found Rome, lived in ancient Latium, near the Tiber River. Populations to the south included the Siculi in Sicily, and the Bruttians, Apulians and Samnites on the mainland. To the north lived the Sabines, Umbrians and Ligurians, among others.

Some of the earliest peoples lived in pile houses along lakes and rivers.

This prehistoric rock painting from northern Italy shows the sun, two axes, knives and a river.

Tiny glass mask from a necklace, made by Carthaginian artisans. The Carthaginians came from the city of Carthage in North Africa. The city was founded in the 8th century BC by Phoenician traders.

Early peoples
Before Rome, the peoples of the Italian peninsula were generally less developed than those of Greece and the rest of the the eastern Mediterranean.

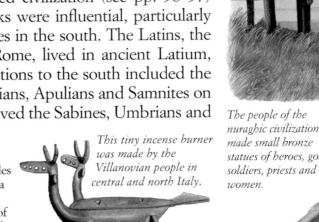

This tiny incense burner was made by the Villanovian people in central and north Italy.

The people of the nuraghic civilization made small bronze statues of heroes, gods, soldiers, priests and women.

The first Sardinians
The earliest inhabitants of the Mediterranean island of Sardinia built strange cone-shaped structures, called nuraghi, made of huge blocks of basalt. Dating from about 1500–400 BC, little is known of the people who built them except that they grew crops and raised livestock.

Contact and trade
Most of the native peoples lived in villages or towns and were farmers. The name *Italia* (Italy) means 'Calf Land'. The Greeks were attracted by the good farmland and by 700 BC several colonies had been established in the south. The peninsula also has rich deposits of metals and both the Greeks and the Phoenicians traded with the Etruscans and other local inhabitants.

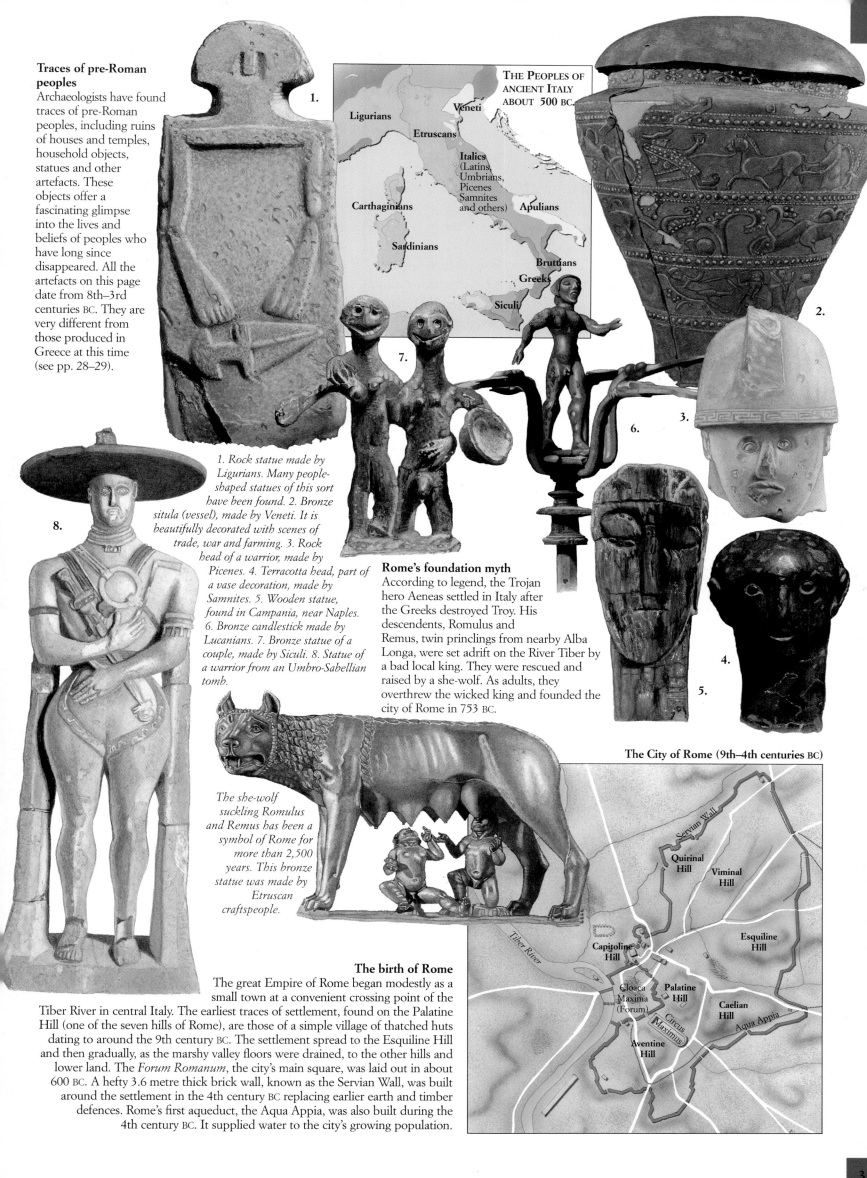

Traces of pre-Roman peoples

Archaeologists have found traces of pre-Roman peoples, including ruins of houses and temples, household objects, statues and other artefacts. These objects offer a fascinating glimpse into the lives and beliefs of peoples who have long since disappeared. All the artefacts on this page date from 8th–3rd centuries BC. They are very different from those produced in Greece at this time (see pp. 28–29).

1.

THE PEOPLES OF ANCIENT ITALY ABOUT 500 BC.

Ligurians
Veneti
Etruscans
Italics (Latins, Umbrians, Picenes Samnites and others)
Carthaginians
Apulians
Sardinians
Bruttians
Greeks
Siculi

2.

3.

6.

8.

7.

4.

5.

1. Rock statue made by Ligurians. Many people-shaped statues of this sort have been found. 2. Bronze situla (vessel), made by Veneti. It is beautifully decorated with scenes of trade, war and farming. 3. Rock head of a warrior, made by Picenes. 4. Terracotta head, part of a vase decoration, made by Samnites. 5. Wooden statue, found in Campania, near Naples. 6. Bronze candlestick made by Lucanians. 7. Bronze statue of a couple, made by Siculi. 8. Statue of a warrior from an Umbro-Sabellian tomb.

Rome's foundation myth

According to legend, the Trojan hero Aeneas settled in Italy after the Greeks destroyed Troy. His descendents, Romulus and Remus, twin princlings from nearby Alba Longa, were set adrift on the River Tiber by a bad local king. They were rescued and raised by a she-wolf. As adults, they overthrew the wicked king and founded the city of Rome in 753 BC.

The she-wolf suckling Romulus and Remus has been a symbol of Rome for more than 2,500 years. This bronze statue was made by Etruscan craftspeople.

The City of Rome (9th–4th centuries BC)

Servian Wall
Quirinal Hill
Viminal Hill
Tiber River
Capitoline Hill
Esquiline Hill
Cloaca Maxima (Forum)
Palatine Hill
Caelian Hill
Circus Maximus
Aqua Appia
Aventine Hill

The birth of Rome

The great Empire of Rome began modestly as a small town at a convenient crossing point of the Tiber River in central Italy. The earliest traces of settlement, found on the Palatine Hill (one of the seven hills of Rome), are those of a simple village of thatched huts dating to around the 9th century BC. The settlement spread to the Esquiline Hill and then gradually, as the marshy valley floors were drained, to the other hills and lower land. The *Forum Romanum*, the city's main square, was laid out in about 600 BC. A hefty 3.6 metre thick brick wall, known as the Servian Wall, was built around the settlement in the 4th century BC replacing earlier earth and timber defences. Rome's first aqueduct, the Aqua Appia, was also built during the 4th century BC. It supplied water to the city's growing population.

The Etruscans

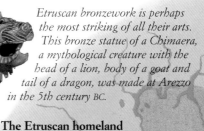

Etruscan bronzework is perhaps the most striking of all their arts. This bronze statue of a Chimaera, a mythological creature with the head of a lion, body of a goat and tail of a dragon, was made at Arezzo in the 5th century BC.

The Etruscan civilization flourished in central Italy for more than 500 years, from about 800–300 BC. It was the first great civilization in the peninsula and it heavily influenced the Romans. Historians are unsure about where the Etruscans originally came from. There are two main, but conflicting, theories, according to which they either migrated to central Italy from west Asia, or were an indigenous people whose civilization developed after contact with the Greeks. In either case, Greek influence was of fundamental importance to the development of Etruscan culture. In turn, the Etruscans passed on many aspects of their culture to the Romans, including the alphabet and writing, religious beliefs and gods, architectural and engineering knowledge, and their peculiar skill as craftspeople and artists. As the power of Rome grew, it gradually eclipsed that of the Etruscans. By the 3rd century BC Etruscan civilization had been absorbed into the Roman Republic.

The Etruscan homeland

The heartland of ancient Etruria lay between the Tiber River in the south and east and the Arno River in the north. In modern Italy this area is still known as Tuscany. During the 7th–6th centuries BC, Etruscan territories stretched north to the Po Valley and south to Campania.

Tinia was the chief Etruscan god. He used three kinds of lightning to enforce his special power.

Etruscan religion

The Etruscans were a deeply religious people. They believed in destiny and the impossibility of changing divine will. Their role was to observe and interpret the gods' messages, present in every aspect of nature. Rules of conduct and religious rites were fulfilled scrupulously.

The Etruscan language

The Etruscan language is written left to right using an alphabet derived from Greek. Even so, Etruscan is not an Indo-European language, nor is it closely related to other known languages. Scholars can now decipher most Etruscan texts, but they still have trouble understanding their meanings. Many words and grammatical forms remain obscure. A large number of texts have been found, but they are mainly short funerary or dedicatory (thanksgiving) inscriptions. Although we know that the Etruscans had their own literature, all traces of it have been lost.

Etruscans made a special type of glossy, black pottery called bucchero. *This bottle-shaped vessel has Etruscan writing on it.*

Linguists have many ways to decipher an unknown language. A common method lies in comparing a text with a translation in a known language. Unfortunately, only a few such bilingual texts have been found in Etruscan. Two gold plaques found in 1964, one in Etruscan (right) and one in Phoenician (left), have been of help, although the two texts are not similar enough to be really useful.

Duck-shaped vessel in Greek red-figure style. Etruscan vase-painting shows strong Greek influence.

Many works of art show married couples banqueting together while reclining comfortably on couches.

Etruscan women

Etruscan women led much freer lives than their counterparts in Greece and Rome. Records show that they owned property and took part in public life alongside the men. They attended sporting events and went to the theatre. Men and women mixed freely at parties, dancing and drinking together.

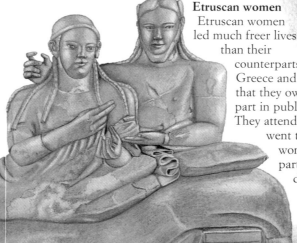

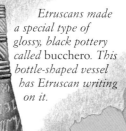

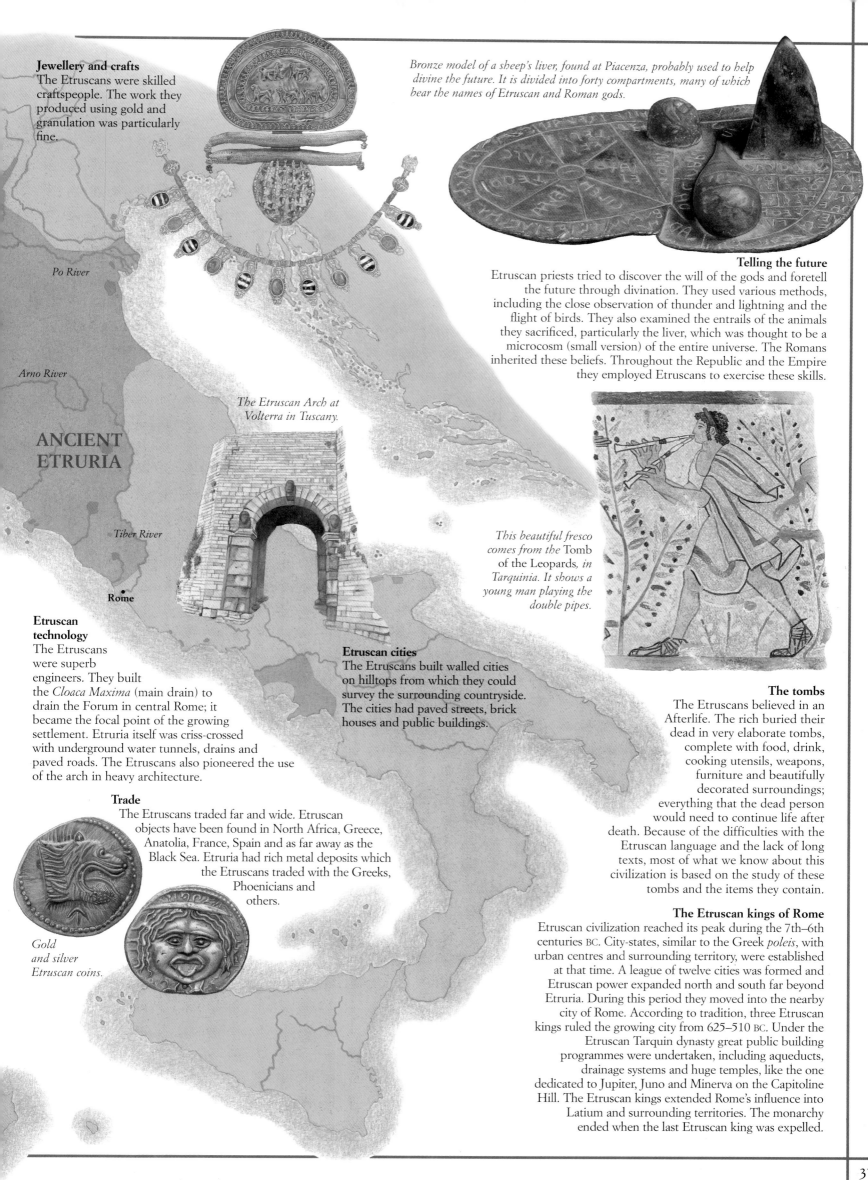

Jewellery and crafts
The Etruscans were skilled craftspeople. The work they produced using gold and granulation was particularly fine.

Bronze model of a sheep's liver, found at Piacenza, probably used to help divine the future. It is divided into forty compartments, many of which bear the names of Etruscan and Roman gods.

Po River

ANCIENT ETRURIA

Arno River

The Etruscan Arch at Volterra in Tuscany.

Tiber River

Rome

Telling the future
Etruscan priests tried to discover the will of the gods and foretell the future through divination. They used various methods, including the close observation of thunder and lightning and the flight of birds. They also examined the entrails of the animals they sacrificed, particularly the liver, which was thought to be a microcosm (small version) of the entire universe. The Romans inherited these beliefs. Throughout the Republic and the Empire they employed Etruscans to exercise these skills.

This beautiful fresco comes from the Tomb of the Leopards, *in Tarquinia. It shows a young man playing the double pipes.*

Etruscan technology
The Etruscans were superb engineers. They built the *Cloaca Maxima* (main drain) to drain the Forum in central Rome; it became the focal point of the growing settlement. Etruria itself was criss-crossed with underground water tunnels, drains and paved roads. The Etruscans also pioneered the use of the arch in heavy architecture.

Etruscan cities
The Etruscans built walled cities on hilltops from which they could survey the surrounding countryside. The cities had paved streets, brick houses and public buildings.

The tombs
The Etruscans believed in an Afterlife. The rich buried their dead in very elaborate tombs, complete with food, drink, cooking utensils, weapons, furniture and beautifully decorated surroundings; everything that the dead person would need to continue life after death. Because of the difficulties with the Etruscan language and the lack of long texts, most of what we know about this civilization is based on the study of these tombs and the items they contain.

Trade
The Etruscans traded far and wide. Etruscan objects have been found in North Africa, Greece, Anatolia, France, Spain and as far away as the Black Sea. Etruria had rich metal deposits which the Etruscans traded with the Greeks, Phoenicians and others.

Gold and silver Etruscan coins.

The Etruscan kings of Rome
Etruscan civilization reached its peak during the 7th–6th centuries BC. City-states, similar to the Greek *poleis*, with urban centres and surrounding territory, were established at that time. A league of twelve cities was formed and Etruscan power expanded north and south far beyond Etruria. During this period they moved into the nearby city of Rome. According to tradition, three Etruscan kings ruled the growing city from 625–510 BC. Under the Etruscan Tarquin dynasty great public building programmes were undertaken, including aqueducts, drainage systems and huge temples, like the one dedicated to Jupiter, Juno and Minerva on the Capitoline Hill. The Etruscan kings extended Rome's influence into Latium and surrounding territories. The monarchy ended when the last Etruscan king was expelled.

The Roman Republic

There are three main periods in Roman history: the Monarchy, the Republic and the Empire. The Etruscan king Tarquin's expulsion from Rome in 509 BC marked the beginning of the Republic. A period of internal struggle followed as the patricians (who had inherited the king's powers) were challenged by the plebians. The patricians consisted of a few wealthy, aristocratic families. They held political power, through the Senate (to which the plebians had no access), as well as civil and religious powers. In time, the plebians won the right to elect their own assembly and magistrates, who represented them in the tribunes. They also won the right for the Republic to have a written code of laws. Other laws limited the power of the patricians and gradually allowed the rise of a wealthy class of plebians. At the same time Rome was almost constantly engaged in a series of expansionist wars with neighbouring lands. By the time the Republic ended in 27 BC, the Romans controlled almost all the territory facing on to the Mediterranean Sea. Julius Caesar conquered Gaul (modern France) in 51 BC, and then journeyed south to Rome with his huge army to proclaim himself dictator of the Roman world. Caesar's murder in 44 BC plunged Rome into a civil war which lasted until Octavian gained the upper hand in 31 BC and made himself Emperor (see pp. 42–43).

The Republic kept Etruscan symbols, including the purple-bordered toga and the bundle of rods with axes (shown here), called the fasces.

This stele comes from the oldest part of the Roman Forum. It bears a religious inscription in Latin. Dating from the 5th century BC, it is the earliest record we have of the Latin language.

The struggle for power
Continual warfare made a number of generals very influential figures in Roman politics. In the 1st century BC, some of them tried to take political power from the Republic. The powerful general Gaius Marius (right) was replaced by Sulla, who made himself dictator.

The Conquest of Italy (until 264 BC)

Conquests until 264 BC

Rome

ADRIATIC SEA

Conquests until 298 BC

TYRRHENIAN SEA

The Roman conquest of the Mediterranean was not without its losses or setbacks. The ferocity of this statue of a Gallic warrior gives us an idea of what the Romans were up against.

The Conquest of the Mediterranean (until 120 BC)

GAUL

GERMANY

SPAIN

DALMATIA

ITALY

Rome

GREECE

ANATOLIA

AFRICA

Carthage

MEDITERRANEAN SEA

King Pyrrhus of Greece used elephants (below) to fight against the Romans when they challenged Greek power in southern Italy.

The conquest of Italy
Rome conquered the Italian peninsula and islands in a series of wars between 437–88 BC. They fought against the Etruscans, Gauls (Rome itself was sacked by the Gauls in 390 BC), Samnites, Greeks, Carthaginians and others.

Samnite warrior.

The Punic Wars
Rome's policy of expansion soon brought it into conflict with another Mediterranean power, the Carthaginians. They first clashed in 264–241 BC in Sicily. Rome won and gained its first overseas colony. In the Second Punic War (218–201 BC) Hannibal invaded Italy from Carthaginian territories in Spain. A second victory brought part of Spain under Roman control. After the Third Punic War (146 BC) Rome annexed the city of Carthage in North Africa and all its territories.

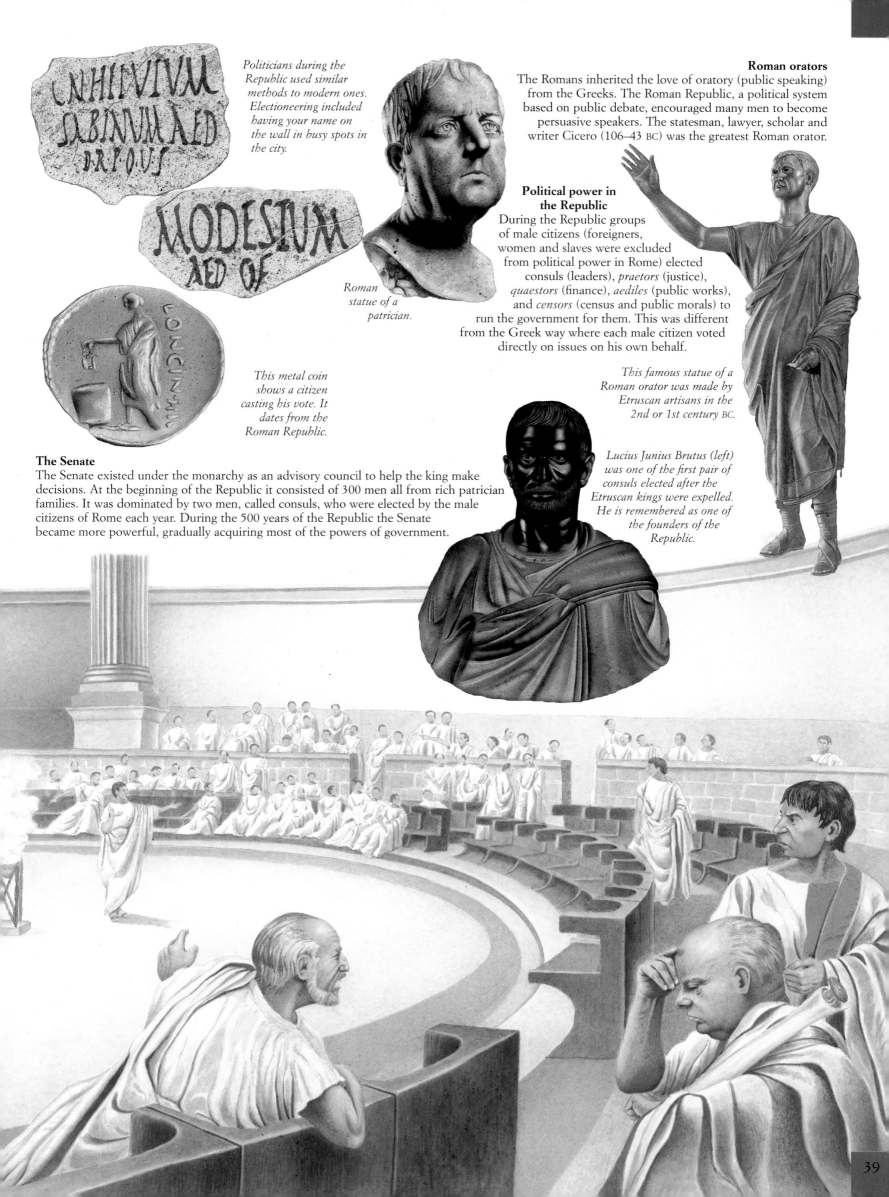

Politicians during the Republic used similar methods to modern ones. Electioneering included having your name on the wall in busy spots in the city.

Roman statue of a patrician.

Roman orators

The Romans inherited the love of oratory (public speaking) from the Greeks. The Roman Republic, a political system based on public debate, encouraged many men to become persuasive speakers. The statesman, lawyer, scholar and writer Cicero (106–43 BC) was the greatest Roman orator.

Political power in the Republic

During the Republic groups of male citizens (foreigners, women and slaves were excluded from political power in Rome) elected consuls (leaders), *praetors* (justice), *quaestors* (finance), *aediles* (public works), and *censors* (census and public morals) to run the government for them. This was different from the Greek way where each male citizen voted directly on issues on his own behalf.

This metal coin shows a citizen casting his vote. It dates from the Roman Republic.

This famous statue of a Roman orator was made by Etruscan artisans in the 2nd or 1st century BC.

The Senate

The Senate existed under the monarchy as an advisory council to help the king make decisions. At the beginning of the Republic it consisted of 300 men all from rich patrician families. It was dominated by two men, called consuls, who were elected by the male citizens of Rome each year. During the 500 years of the Republic the Senate became more powerful, gradually acquiring most of the powers of government.

Lucius Junius Brutus (left) was one of the first pair of consuls elected after the Etruscan kings were expelled. He is remembered as one of the founders of the Republic.

The Roman Army

Rome became a great Empire because it had a huge, well-organized army. It was composed of a citizen army (the legions), auxiliary troops (non-Romans), and a large naval fleet stationed in coastal cities. There was also the Praetorian Guard, which was the emperor's bodyguard. The legions were either stationed near the Empire's frontiers, where their presence alone acted as a warning against invasion, or in strategic areas of conquered territories from which they could control the local people. When soldiers were not actively involved in war – which was more often than not – they lived like ordinary citizens as farmers or traders. Even when stationed far from Rome, they expected (and built) all the amenities of a Roman town, including baths, amphitheatres and aqueducts. This helped make Roman culture a permanent feature of even outlying areas.

The legions carried standards like the one shown here. It was usually a wooden javelin with a pointed tip, decorated with an eagle (symbol of Jupiter), golden crowns (awarded to the first soldiers to climb enemy walls) and signs of the zodiac.

A Legionary's equipment
Besides his heavy armour and helmet, a legionary usually carried a javelin, a double-edged sword, and a heavy shield. On the march he also carried a thick woollen cloak, a saw, a basket, a pickaxe, a chain, a leather thong, a sickle and three days' food rations.

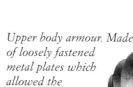

Metal helmet. The design changed many times, but all models protected the head, face and neck, leaving the eyes and ears free.

Upper body armour. Made of loosely fastened metal plates which allowed the soldier to move.

A woollen tunic reaching to the knees was worn under the armour.

Heavy leather belt, studded with metal.

Legionaries signed up for twenty years. On discharge, they could choose between a lump sum payment or a piece of land. Most chose the land and settled down as small farmers.

Wooden shield. The large, rectangular shield was curved to protect the soldier's body. It had a leather strap behind so that it could be carried while on the march.

Slavery
There were many slaves in ancient Roman society. Historians estimate that over one-third of the population was made up of slaves. Many slaves were the defeated citizens of territories conquered by the Roman army. For example, at least 50,000 Carthaginians were enslaved at the end of the Punic Wars in 146 BC. Slaves were widely employed as agricultural labourers, domestic helpers and to work in workshops, factories and mines.

The legions
Legionaries were highly trained, well equipped foot soldiers. They were the backbone of the Roman army. Only Roman citizens were allowed to join the legions. There were about 5,000 men in each (the number varied from period to period) and the army had anywhere between 25 and 35 legions (once again, depending on the period). Each legion was divided into groups called centuries whose commander was called a centurion. Six centuries made up a cohort and ten cohorts a legion.

The auxiliaries
The auxiliaries were recruited from non-Roman peoples living within the Empire. They were organized in cohorts of 500 or 1,000 soldiers under the command of a Roman officer. They were less well paid than legionaries and served for a longer period, but received Roman citizenship on discharge.

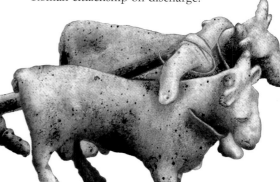

Roman warships carried troops and had a gangway which could be lowered when they were alongside an enemy ship.

The navy
Rome had only a tiny fleet before the Punic Wars, but they quickly built up a large navy after facing the seafaring Cathaginians. The Emperor Augustus enlarged the navy, establishing permanent fleets of warships based at Naples and Ravenna and sending others into the Mediterranean and Black seas. A part of their job was to watch out for and eliminate pirates. The navy also had troop and supply carriers which could travel by sea or river.

Like Greek ships (see pp. 20–21), Roman vessels were also equipped with a ram.

Siege towers
Roman engineers constructed huge siege towers which they used to breach the walls of fortresses. The lower stories housed a huge battering ram with a pointed head for breaching or a ram-shaped head for battering. In the upper stories archers shot arrows at the enemy soldiers on the ramparts. The towers were sometimes as tall as 50 metres.

Defending the frontiers in Europe
The Empire was under constant pressure from Germanic peoples in northern Europe. The frontier ran along the Rhine and the Danube rivers which formed a natural barrier so there was no need for a continuous wall like the one in northern Britain. However, forts, camps and watchtowers were built along the southern banks of both rivers and a standing army was deployed to discourage attack.

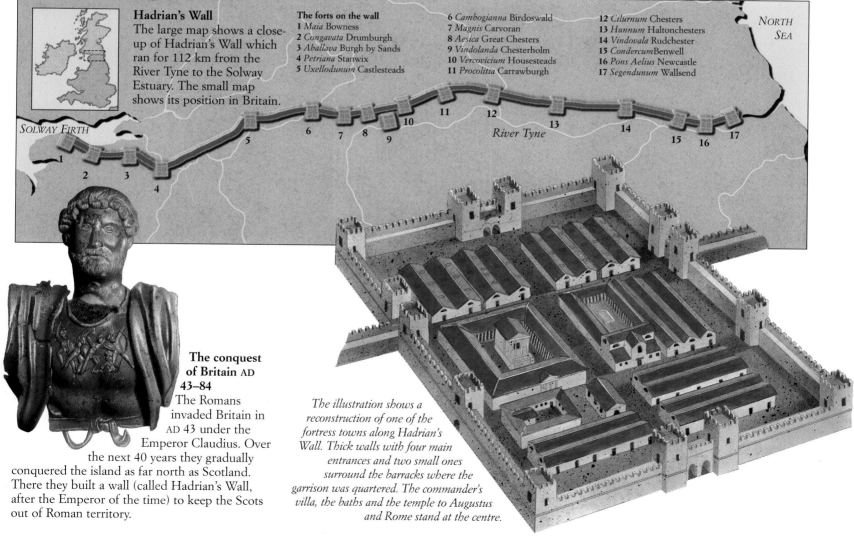

Hadrian's Wall
The large map shows a close-up of Hadrian's Wall which ran for 112 km from the River Tyne to the Solway Estuary. The small map shows its position in Britain.

The forts on the wall
1 *Maia* Bowness
2 *Congavata* Drumburgh
3 *Aballava* Burgh by Sands
4 *Petriana* Stanwix
5 *Uxellodunun* Castlesteads
6 *Cambogianna* Birdoswald
7 *Magnis* Carvoran
8 *Aesica* Great Chesters
9 *Vindolanda* Chesterholm
10 *Vercovicium* Housesteads
11 *Procolitia* Carrawburgh
12 *Cilurnum* Chesters
13 *Hunnum* Haltonchesters
14 *Vindovala* Rudchester
15 *Condercum* Benwell
16 *Pons Aelius* Newcastle
17 *Segendunum* Wallsend

NORTH SEA

SOLWAY FIRTH

River Tyne

The conquest of Britain AD 43–84
The Romans invaded Britain in AD 43 under the Emperor Claudius. Over the next 40 years they gradually conquered the island as far north as Scotland. There they built a wall (called Hadrian's Wall, after the Emperor of the time) to keep the Scots out of Roman territory.

The illustration shows a reconstruction of one of the fortress towns along Hadrian's Wall. Thick walls with four main entrances and two small ones surround the barracks where the garrison was quartered. The commander's villa, the baths and the temple to Augustus and Rome stand at the centre.

Britain

By the end of the 1st century AD most of Britain was under Roman rule (see p. 41). A huge army consisting of three legions (15,000 men) and 40,000 auxiliaries was permanently stationed there. Roman citizenship was granted to many Britons after they had served in the auxiliaries. Romanization of the locals was strongest in the towns and among the upper classes. Many rural peasants continued to speak Celtic and maintained their traditional culture.

Before the Romans conquered Britain the people were of mainly Celtic origin. Celtic craftspeople made this inlaid shield (above) in the 1st century BC.

The Maison Carrée in Nimes (northern France) is a perfect example of a Corinthian temple. Dating from the time of Augustus, it is one of the best preserved of Roman monuments. It is now used as an exhibition centre.

The Porta Nigra, the northern gate of the Roman city of Trier. Built in the 3rd century, it was later converted into a church.

The success of Roman colonization

The Romans acquired and maintained their Empire through military might. But they also encouraged the peoples they conquered to take part in Roman life. Many became Roman citizens. In the later Empire many of the Emperors were not of Italian origin.

Gaul

Ancient Gaul, inhabited by the Celtic Gauls, covered modern France and parts of Belgium, Germany and northern Italy. Julius Caesar conquered Gaul, bringing it under the Roman yolk in 50 BC. In AD 260 Gaul, Spain and Britain revolted, forming an independent Gallic empire governed from Trier. Aurelian brought the area back into the Empire.

Coin with a Gallic warrior. For a long time it was thought to show Vercingetorix, the leader of a revolt against Caesar in 53 BC.

Roman Spain

Southern Spain came under Roman power during the Punic Wars. The north was conquered in 19 BC. Spain was divided into three provinces. It was a wealthy area, with great cities and a thriving export trade. Wine, olive oil, fish sauce, gold, copper and silver were the main exports. Two great Roman Emperors, Trajan and Hadrian, were of Spanish origin.

Medusa medallion from Leptis Magna. The city reached the height of its splendour during the reign of Septimius Severus, who was born there in AD 146.

Bust of Julius Caesar (100–44 BC). Statesman, general and, during the last four years of his life, dictator of Republican Rome.

Poetry and literature

Augustus and other wealthy Romans felt that patronage of the arts was part of their duty as first citizens. They encouraged and supported many poets and historians. The early Empire was a golden age in Latin literature; Horace, Virgil and Livy were all working at this time. Virgil's epic poem *Aeneid*, which tells of the founding of Rome by Aeneas of Troy and the greatness of Augustan rule, is still regarded as a masterpiece. In the same period Pliny the Elder wrote his enormous encyclopaedia called *Natural History*. Vitruvius wrote a treatise on architecture which was very important for the revival of Classical architecture during the Renaissance nearly fourteen centuries later.

Relief showing Pompeii during the earthquake in AD 62.

Pompeii

The southern Italian city of Pompeii was destroyed in AD 79 when Mount Vesuvius erupted. The city, buried in volcanic rock until archaeologists dug it up again, has been an important source of information on daily life in a Roman town.

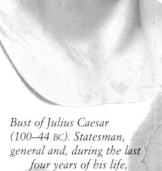

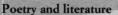

BRITANNIA

Londinium (London)

GALLIA

DALMAT

ITALIA

Rome

HISPANIA

Carthage

Hadrumetum

Leptis Magna

The Roman Empire

The Empire was established in 27 BC when the Roman general Octavian, who had defeated the last of his rivals in 31 BC, accepted the title of 'Augustus' and became the first Emperor. Augustus was a shrewd ruler; while keeping all power in his own hands, he allowed the Senate and the Republican ruling classes to share with him in administering the Empire. Augustus introduced far-reaching reforms which improved family and social life, lowered taxation, limited corruption and revived traditional religious cults. He also extended the frontiers, making the Empire larger than ever. His rule introduced a period of peace and stable government which lasted for around 200 years. It was only interrupted by brief periods of unrest, usually caused by discord regarding the succession of a new emperor. The period is known as the *Pax Romana* (Roman peace).

The northern frontiers

Augustus pushed the frontier in the Alps and the Balkans north as far as the Danube River. Further west, he advanced north beyond the Rhine River to the Elbe. His stepson Drusus fought successful campaigns from 12 BC. But disaster struck in 9 BC when three legions (about 15,000 men) were ambushed and slaughtered in the Teutonburg Forest. The Roman frontier was pulled back to the Rhine, where it stayed until the fall of the Empire.

The Tropaeum Traiani, built in AD 109 in Dacia to celebrate Trajan's victories over the Dacians. Trajan's column in Rome was built to celebrate the same victory.

Augustus (63 BC–AD 14), the first Roman Emperor. Augustus was commander-in-chief of the Roman armies. This statue shows him in full military dress.

DACIA

Greece

The Romans conquered Greece in 146 BC. Apart from an unsuccessful revolt in 88 BC, the Greeks lived peacefully under Roman rule.

Byzantium

ANATOLIA

GREECE

Athens

Ephesus

The temple of Artemis at Ephesus, with its statue of the goddess (right), was much visited by pilgrims.

MEDITERRANEAN SEA

The eastern provinces

Rome took control of Asia Minor (modern Turkey) and the Levant (modern Syria, Lebanon and Israel) in the 2nd and 1st centuries BC. These were wealthy areas with developed urban cultures. Greek had been the common language since Alexander the Great's invasion. Roman civilization absorbed much from these provinces, including Christianity.

Antioch

One of the famous Fayyum portraits (below). Reflecting an interesting mix of Roman pictorial style and Egyptian funerary culture, these portraits were painted on wood or linen and placed over the faces of dead people.

Trajan's wars

The Emperor Trajan, who ruled from AD 98–117, extended the frontiers again. In 105 he conquered the Dacian kingdom (modern Romania). In 114 he moved east, campaigning against Rome's main rivals, the Parthian Empire. Under Trajan, Rome briefly held territory as far east as Mesopotamia and the Persian Gulf.

Tigris River

Euphrates River

Persian Gulf

Egypt

Augustus took personal control of Egypt after Cleopatra's suicide in 31 BC. Roman culture had less influence in Egypt than elsewhere, whereas Egyptian art and religion had quite an impact on the Roman world. For example, the cults of Isis, Osiris and Serapis were common in Rome. The fertile lands of the Nile grew cereals. Egypt also exported luxury goods.

Alexandria

Nile River

North Africa

The African provinces stretched from the Atlantic Ocean to Egypt and the Red Sea. The fertile lands were used to grow olives and cereals, most of which were exported. It was a wealthy area and the local people lived well. Large cities, such as Carthage, Thysdrus and Leptis Magna flourished. Because of its situation between the Mediterranean Sea and the Sahara Desert, North Africa was not threatened by invasion. Although a system of forts was built, only one legion was stationed in Africa, compared with fourteen or more on the Rhine–Danube frontier in the north.

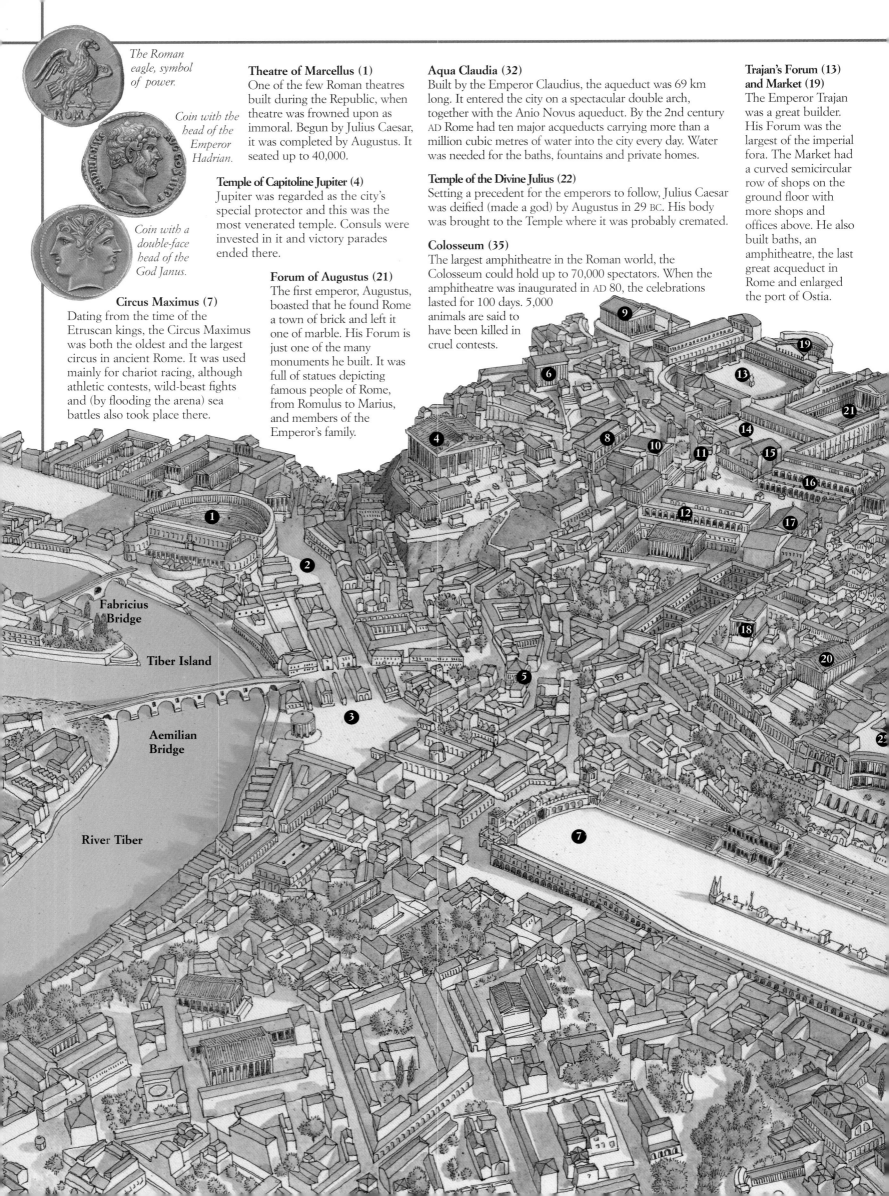

The Roman eagle, symbol of power.

Coin with the head of the Emperor Hadrian.

Coin with a double-face head of the God Janus.

Theatre of Marcellus (1)
One of the few Roman theatres built during the Republic, when theatre was frowned upon as immoral. Begun by Julius Caesar, it was completed by Augustus. It seated up to 40,000.

Temple of Capitoline Jupiter (4)
Jupiter was regarded as the city's special protector and this was the most venerated temple. Consuls were invested in it and victory parades ended there.

Forum of Augustus (21)
The first emperor, Augustus, boasted that he found Rome a town of brick and left it one of marble. His Forum is just one of the many monuments he built. It was full of statues depicting famous people of Rome, from Romulus to Marius, and members of the Emperor's family.

Circus Maximus (7)
Dating from the time of the Etruscan kings, the Circus Maximus was both the oldest and the largest circus in ancient Rome. It was used mainly for chariot racing, although athletic contests, wild-beast fights and (by flooding the arena) sea battles also took place there.

Aqua Claudia (32)
Built by the Emperor Claudius, the aqueduct was 69 km long. It entered the city on a spectacular double arch, together with the Anio Novus aqueduct. By the 2nd century AD Rome had ten major acqueducts carrying more than a million cubic metres of water into the city every day. Water was needed for the baths, fountains and private homes.

Temple of the Divine Julius (22)
Setting a precedent for the emperors to follow, Julius Caesar was deified (made a god) by Augustus in 29 BC. His body was brought to the Temple where it was probably cremated.

Colosseum (35)
The largest amphitheatre in the Roman world, the Colosseum could hold up to 70,000 spectators. When the amphitheatre was inaugurated in AD 80, the celebrations lasted for 100 days. 5,000 animals are said to have been killed in cruel contests.

Trajan's Forum (13) and Market (19)
The Emperor Trajan was a great builder. His Forum was the largest of the imperial fora. The Market had a curved semicircular row of shops on the ground floor with more shops and offices above. He also built baths, an amphitheatre, the last great acqueduct in Rome and enlarged the port of Ostia.

Fabricius Bridge

Tiber Island

Aemilian Bridge

River Tiber

The City of Rome

Between the 1st and 4th centuries AD Rome had a population of about one million people. It was a magnificent city, with forums, theatres, amphitheatres, circuses, baths, temples, triumphal arches and columns and aqueducts built by the various emperors. Rich people lived in splendid palaces which had running water and underfloor heating. The middle classes (craftspeople, doctors, magicians, teachers, merchants, shopkeepers and others) lived comfortably in houses or blocks of flats. There was also a large population of poor people and slaves, many of whom lived in appalling conditions. Wheat, oil and other basic necessities were distributed free to keep them from revolting.

Caput Mundi
Capital of the World

When the Etruscans were building the temple of Capitoline Jupiter they uncovered a human skull. They interpreted this as a sign that Rome would become the capital of the world. By the 1st century AD Rome was the capital of an Empire that governed 50 million people on three different continents.

KEY TO ILLUSTRATION

1. Theatre of Marcellus
2. Forum Holitorium (produce market)
3. Forum Boarium (cattle market)
4. Temple of Jupiter Capitolinus
5. Arch of Janus
6. Temple of Juno Moneta
7. Circus Maximus
8. Tablarium
9. Temple of the Divine Trajan
10. Temple of Concord
11. Arch of Septimius Severus
12. Basilica Julia
13. Forum of Trajan
14. Forum of Caesar
15. Curia
16. Basilica Aemilia
17. Temple of Castor and Pollux
18. Temple of Cybele
19. Markets of Trajan
20. Temple of Apollo
21. Forum of Augustus
22. Temple of the Divine Julius
23. Forum of Vespasian
24. Basilica of Maxentius
25. Imperial Palace
26. Domus Augustana
27. Domus Flavia
28. Temple of Venus and Rome
29. Temple of the Caesars
30. Palace of Septimius Severus
31. Septizonium
32. Aqua Claudia
33. Arch of Constantine
34. Colossus of Nero
35. Colosseum
36. School of the gladiators
37. Temple of the Divine Claudius
38. Aqua Marcia

The illustration below shows a large part of central Rome and many of its most important monuments during the 4th century AD.

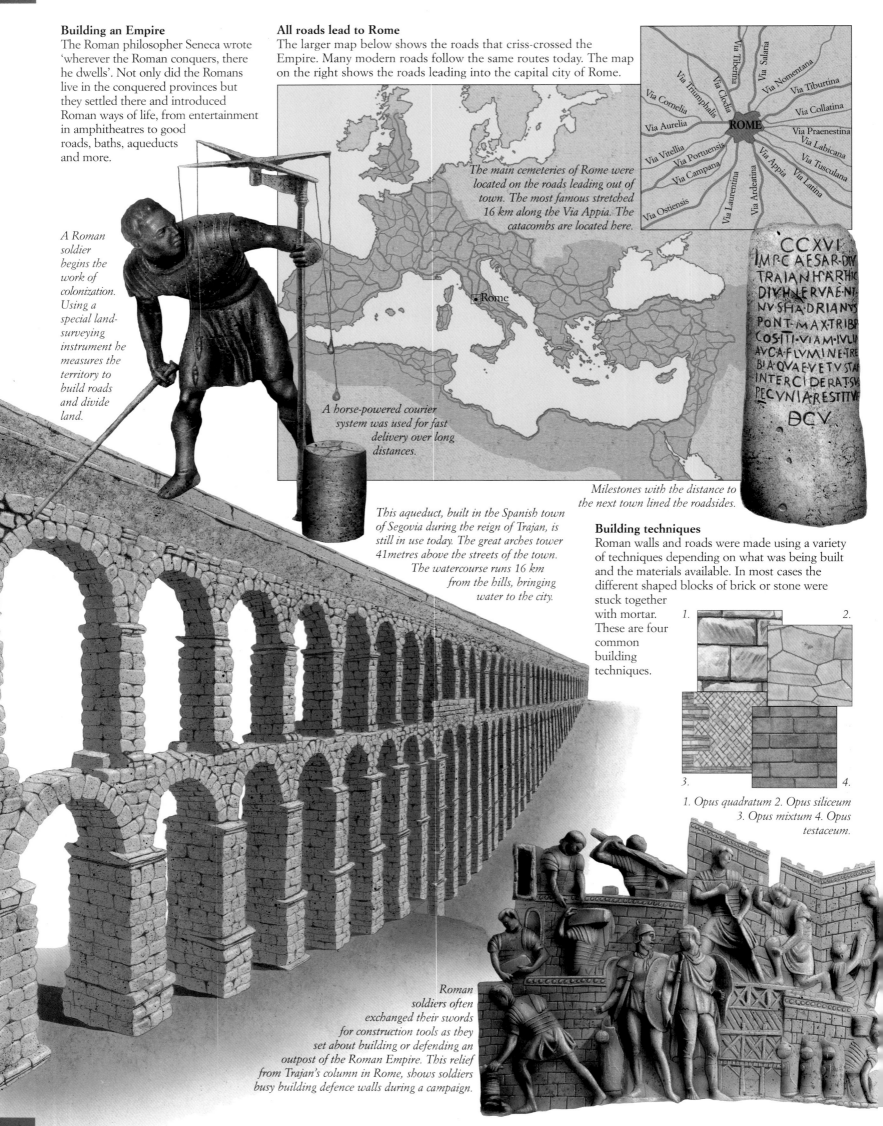

Building an Empire

The Roman philosopher Seneca wrote 'wherever the Roman conquers, there he dwells'. Not only did the Romans live in the conquered provinces but they settled there and introduced Roman ways of life, from entertainment in amphitheatres to good roads, baths, aqueducts and more.

A Roman soldier begins the work of colonization. Using a special land-surveying instrument he measures the territory to build roads and divide land.

All roads lead to Rome

The larger map below shows the roads that criss-crossed the Empire. Many modern roads follow the same routes today. The map on the right shows the roads leading into the capital city of Rome.

The main cemeteries of Rome were located on the roads leading out of town. The most famous stretched 16 km along the Via Appia. The catacombs are located here.

Via Tiberina · Via Salaria · Via Triumphalis · Via Clodia · Via Nomentana · Via Cornelia · Via Tiburtina · Via Aurelia · Via Collatina · **ROME** · Via Praenestina · Via Vitellia · Via Portuensis · Via Labicana · Via Campana · Via Tusculana · Via Laurentina · Via Appia · Via Latina · Via Ostiensis · Via Ardeatina

Rome

A horse-powered courier system was used for fast delivery over long distances.

CCXVI
IMPC AESAR·DIV
TRAIAN H·ARHIC
DIVH·ERVAE·NT
NVSHADRIANVS
PONT·MAX·TRIBP
COSTI·VIAM·IVLIA
AVCA·FLVMINE·TRE
BIA·QVA·E·VETVSTA
INTERCIDERAT·SV
PECVNIA·RESTITVE
DCV

Milestones with the distance to the next town lined the roadsides.

This aqueduct, built in the Spanish town of Segovia during the reign of Trajan, is still in use today. The great arches tower 41metres above the streets of the town. The watercourse runs 16 km from the hills, bringing water to the city.

Building techniques

Roman walls and roads were made using a variety of techniques depending on what was being built and the materials available. In most cases the different shaped blocks of brick or stone were stuck together with mortar. These are four common building techniques.

1. 2. 3. 4.

1. Opus quadratum 2. Opus siliceum 3. Opus mixtum 4. Opus testaceum.

Roman soldiers often exchanged their swords for construction tools as they set about building or defending an outpost of the Roman Empire. This relief from Trajan's column in Rome, shows soldiers busy building defence walls during a campaign.

This beautifully carved cameo shows four portraits, of the Emperor Claudius with his wife Agrippina the Younger and Germanicus with his wife Agrippina the Elder.

Glass, gems, and jewellery

The secrets of producing high quality decorative glass spread from Syria to Italy and the Rhineland (Germany). Glass-blowing became the quickest and cheapest method of production and vessels and decorative items were produced in both plain and coloured glass. During the Republic there were limits on the amount of jewellery a person could wear. These restrictions were lifted during the Empire and rich Roman women adorned themselves with necklaces, rings, earrings, bracelets and hair ornaments.

Wall paintings and portraits

Roman artists used a mixture of hot beeswax and pigments to paint realistic portraits like the one shown here of Terentius Neo and his wife, from Pompeii (southern Italy). They also used fresco technique to paint directly on to walls. Only a few of these beautiful paintings have survived.

The art of mosaic

The Romans created decorative pavements and panels using roughly shaped cubes of stones, tiles or glass fitted together to make a scene or pattern. Since the materials for mosaics were cheap and easy-to-find, the art was widely used throughout the Empire. Mosaics could be brightly coloured, like the one shown here, or in black and white.

Roman sculpture

In portrait sculpture, the Romans preferred a more realistic, warts-and-all approach than the Greeks. The busts of many statesmen, with their cropped hair and shrewd expressions, are telling portraits of the ruthless men who ran the Empire.

Roman portrait statue of an unknown citizen.

Medicine

Many Greek doctors moved to Rome. One Greek, called Galen, who practised in Rome after AD 161, was the first to realize that human arteries are full of blood and not air. Compared with Greece, the Roman contribution to medicine lay more in the area of public health than theoretical knowledge. The Roman state ensured the supply of fresh water to cities, made gymnasiums and baths available to all, and provided good sewage disposal.

A Roman oculist attends to a patient.

Technology and Art

Roman art was strongly influenced by Greek art from earliest times. During the Republic when the Romans sacked the Greek towns of southern Italy and mainland Greece, statues and other items poured into Rome. Wealthy Romans amassed great collections. They also imported Greek artists and craftspeople to create new items in the Greek style. However, new subject matter and the Roman character did lead to a new Graeco-Roman style of art. In a similar way the Romans were influenced by Greek and Etruscan technology, although in this case they went far beyond the achievements of their predecessors. Master engineers and builders, wherever they conquered, they settled and built. By way of their technology, they introduced the local inhabitants to a Roman lifestyle and united all the peoples of the Empire in a common culture. Modern Europe, North Africa and the Near East are still dotted with the remains of roads, triumphal arches, temples, baths, bridges and others remnants of Roman civilization.

Blue Vase, in blue glass with white glass decorations, from Pompeii.

Roman Daily Life

The history of Rome covers a period of almost a 1,000 years and includes peoples from England and northern Europe, Africa, the Mediterranean and the Near East. People lived differently according to where they were born and at which time. This spread looks at daily life in a typical town in Italy or southern Europe during the Republican and Imperial ages. The family was the mainstay in Roman society and consisted of the *pater familias* (father and head of the family), mother, children, other relatives and slaves. The father had complete authority over the others, even to the point of authorizing their enslavement or deaths. Society was divided into citizens (patricians and plebians), freemen (freed slaves) and slaves. A large proportion of the population was made up of slaves.

A Roman matron baths her child with the help of a female relative or slave.

In the early years of Roman history, fathers taught their children to read and write.

Roman women

After just a few years of schooling, girls stayed at home to learn domestic work. They were married young to much older husbands. Wealthy matrons rarely left the house unless accompanied by a male member of the family or a slave. Married women had no political rights, but they often accompanied their husbands into society and were a little freer than Greek women.

Food

The mass of Roman people ate frugal meals, based on cereals, bread, beans, oil, a little meat or fish and fruit. Wealthy Romans are famous for their sumptuous banquets where elaborate dishes such as flamingos' tongues, mullets' livers and wild boar stuffed with live thrushes were served.

This relief shows a slave woman in a butcher's shop. Shopping was one of the best jobs for a domestic slave; she was out of her mistresses' sight, in the fresh air, chatting with others of her kind.

Education

Wealthy boys and girls went to school from about the age of seven. After they were about twelve, only the boys went on to study with a *grammaticus* (tutor) who taught them literature and history. Poor children worked from a young age.

A gold bulla. Children wore bullae and other charms around their necks to protect them from evil.

Relief of a tiny shop with a craftsman offering his knives and choppers for sale.

Bread

Bread became a staple food during the imperial period. Before then the people ate a kind of polenta (rather like porridge) made of barley.

Housing

Rich Romans lived in spacious houses with beautiful mosaic floors, elegant furniture, rugs and wall paintings. However, the majority of city-dwellers lived in large apartment blocks, called *insulae*. The lower floors had shops opening on to the street. Many of the apartments were small, cramped and dark. Glass for windows only became widespread after the 1st century AD.

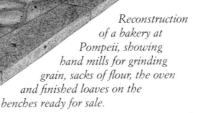

Reconstruction of a bakery at Pompeii, showing hand mills for grinding grain, sacks of flour, the oven and finished loaves on the benches ready for sale.

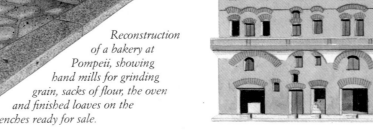

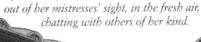

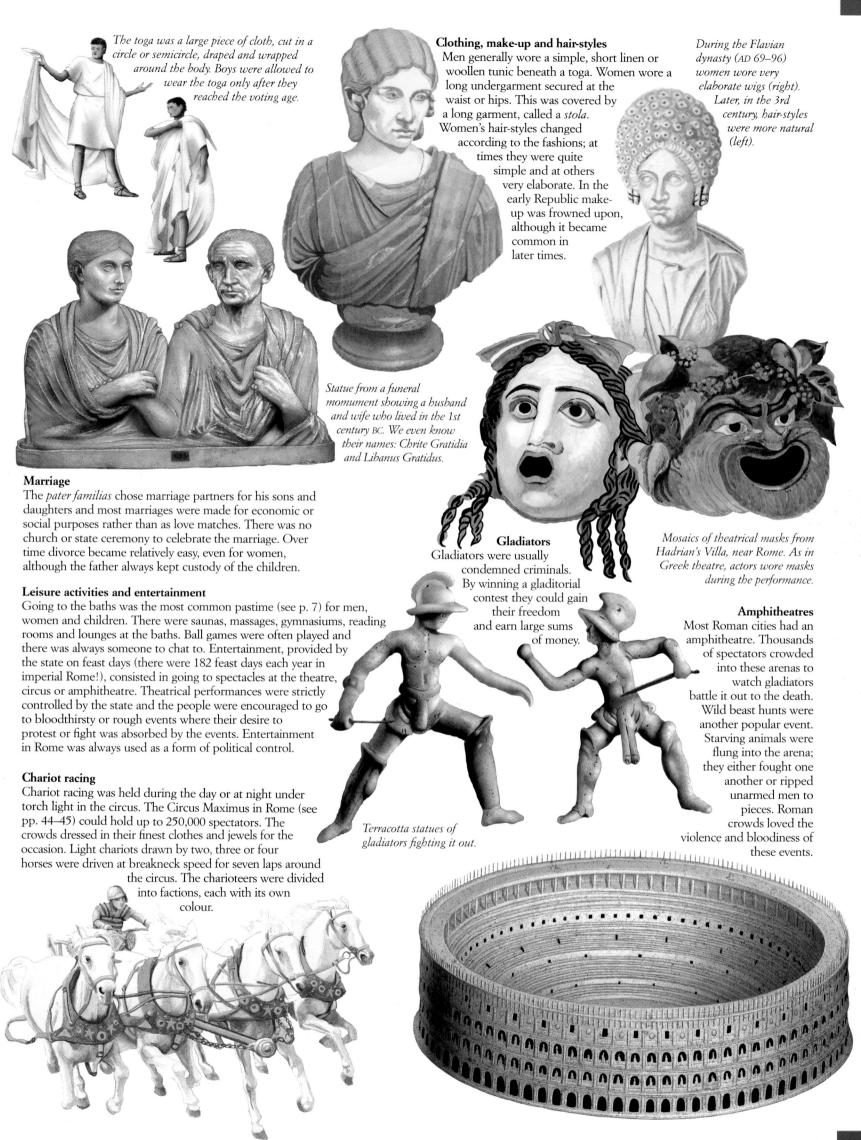

The toga was a large piece of cloth, cut in a circle or semicircle, draped and wrapped around the body. Boys were allowed to wear the toga only after they reached the voting age.

Clothing, make-up and hair-styles

Men generally wore a simple, short linen or woollen tunic beneath a toga. Women wore a long undergarment secured at the waist or hips. This was covered by a long garment, called a *stola*. Women's hair-styles changed according to the fashions; at times they were quite simple and at others very elaborate. In the early Republic make-up was frowned upon, although it became common in later times.

During the Flavian dynasty (AD 69–96) women wore very elaborate wigs (right). Later, in the 3rd century, hair-styles were more natural (left).

Statue from a funeral momument showing a husband and wife who lived in the 1st century BC. We even know their names: Chrite Gratidia and Libanus Gratidus.

Marriage

The *pater familias* chose marriage partners for his sons and daughters and most marriages were made for economic or social purposes rather than as love matches. There was no church or state ceremony to celebrate the marriage. Over time divorce became relatively easy, even for women, although the father always kept custody of the children.

Leisure activities and entertainment

Going to the baths was the most common pastime (see p. 7) for men, women and children. There were saunas, massages, gymnasiums, reading rooms and lounges at the baths. Ball games were often played and there was always someone to chat to. Entertainment, provided by the state on feast days (there were 182 feast days each year in imperial Rome!), consisted in going to spectacles at the theatre, circus or amphitheatre. Theatrical performances were strictly controlled by the state and the people were encouraged to go to bloodthirsty or rough events where their desire to protest or fight was absorbed by the events. Entertainment in Rome was always used as a form of political control.

Chariot racing

Chariot racing was held during the day or at night under torch light in the circus. The Circus Maximus in Rome (see pp. 44–45) could hold up to 250,000 spectators. The crowds dressed in their finest clothes and jewels for the occasion. Light chariots drawn by two, three or four horses were driven at breakneck speed for seven laps around the circus. The charioteers were divided into factions, each with its own colour.

Gladiators

Gladiators were usually condemned criminals. By winning a gladitorial contest they could gain their freedom and earn large sums of money.

Terracotta statues of gladiators fighting it out.

Mosaics of theatrical masks from Hadrian's Villa, near Rome. As in Greek theatre, actors wore masks during the performance.

Amphitheatres

Most Roman cities had an amphitheatre. Thousands of spectators crowded into these arenas to watch gladiators battle it out to the death. Wild beast hunts were another popular event. Starving animals were flung into the arena; they either fought one another or ripped unarmed men to pieces. Roman crowds loved the violence and bloodiness of these events.

Roman Religion

Sanctuary dedicated to the mythical Aeneas of Troy, ancestor of Romulus and Remus.

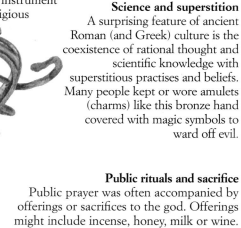

Pottery funery urn from the 9th century BC in the form of a hut. The ashes of the dead were buried in these urns.

The Romans worshipped many gods. Some were native to Italy and others came from the lands they conquered. Roman religion, with its roots in a rural world of shepherds and farmers, was a practical affair from the start. The idea was to keep peace with the gods. Being in favour with a spirit or god could increase yields at harvest time or protect the family and home from misfortune. There were gods for every aspect of life, each of which could be worshipped or sacrificed to, in return for favours or information about the future. Early beliefs in divinities of fire, water and wind gave way to those in gods with human characteristics. City-dwellers built temples to the various gods and made them offerings, including the sacrifice of animals. As the Roman Empire expanded, it absorbed many of the religious beliefs and forms of worship of the peoples it conquered. For example, the Greek gods Zeus, Hera, Athena and Dionysus became the Roman gods Jupiter, Juno, Minerva and Bacchus. Other gods adopted from abroad included Mithras from Persia, Cybele from Anatolia and Isis from Egypt. From the time of Augustus the emperor was also recognized as a divine being. The Jewish and Christian religions spread through the Empire from the 1st century AD. Followers of both religions were persecuted because their beliefs were monotheistic (recognizing only one god). In AD 312 the Emperor Constantine was converted to Christianity and in AD 313, by the Edict of Milan, he made it the official state religion.

Ancestor worship
This Roman patrician is holding masks of his ancestors. Wax masks of ancestors were carried during funeral processions.

The cult of Isis
Isis was one of the most important goddesses of ancient Egypt. Her cult spread to Greece and Rome. The sistrum (below) is a musical instrument traditionally used during religious meetings in her honour.

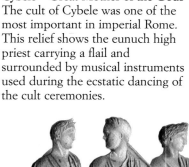

Science and superstition
A surprising feature of ancient Roman (and Greek) culture is the coexistence of rational thought and scientific knowledge with superstitious practises and beliefs. Many people kept or wore amulets (charms) like this bronze hand covered with magic symbols to ward off evil.

Cybele – Great Mother of the Gods
The cult of Cybele was one of the most important in imperial Rome. This relief shows the eunuch high priest carrying a flail and surrounded by musical instruments used during the ecstatic dancing of the cult ceremonies.

Public rituals and sacrifice
Public prayer was often accompanied by offerings or sacrifices to the god. Offerings might include incense, honey, milk or wine. One of the most frequent sacrifices involved the killing of a pig, a sheep and an ox. The internal organs of the animals were cooked, chopped up and left on the altar for the god. The rest of the animals was consumed at a sacrificial banquet.

Household religion
The *pater familias* was also the family priest and had to ensure that the Lares and Penates (household gods) were worshipped. A prayer was said to them each morning and special offerings were made at family festivals.

Statue of the Emperor Claudius as the god Jupiter.

The most important Mithraic ceremony was the slaying of the bull. The bull's blood was thought to fertilize all vegetation.

Christianity

The new Christian religion spread slowly during the 1st and 2nd centuries. Persecution of Christians began after the great fire that devastated the capital during Nero's reign in AD 64. The Christians were blamed for causing this and other misfortunes because they refused to worship the emperor and sacrifice to the state gods. The Romans thought this made the other gods angry, causing them to inflict fire and misfortune as punishment.

The cult of Mithras

The worship of Mithras, god of the sun, justice, contracts and war, came from Persia (modern Iran). This religion became very popular in the Roman world during the 2nd century AD where it was the chief rival to the Christian religion. Mithraism was a religion of loyalty toward the king. It was encouraged by many emperors, and took root particularly among soldiers.

The dome of the Pantheon rises to 43 metres above the ground. A masterpiece of engineering, architects are still not sure exactly how it was constructed. Inside, the temple is flooded by light which pours in through an opening in the ceiling eight metres in diameter. Decorated with coloured marble, the impact of this ancient building is unforgettable.

Jesus shown as the Good Shepherd, from the catacomb of Priscilla in Rome.

Emperor worship

From the time of the first emperor Augustus, Romans were encouraged to view and worship their emperor as a god. The Empire, so vast and diverse, needed a divine emperor as a central figure and focus of loyalty. Temples dedicated to the emperor sprang up all over the Empire.

The Pantheon

The Pantheon is the best preserved of all the ancient Roman buildings. Built almost nineteen centuries ago and dedicated to all the gods (it is still in use as a Christian church), it gives us some idea of the grandeur of the Roman achievement.

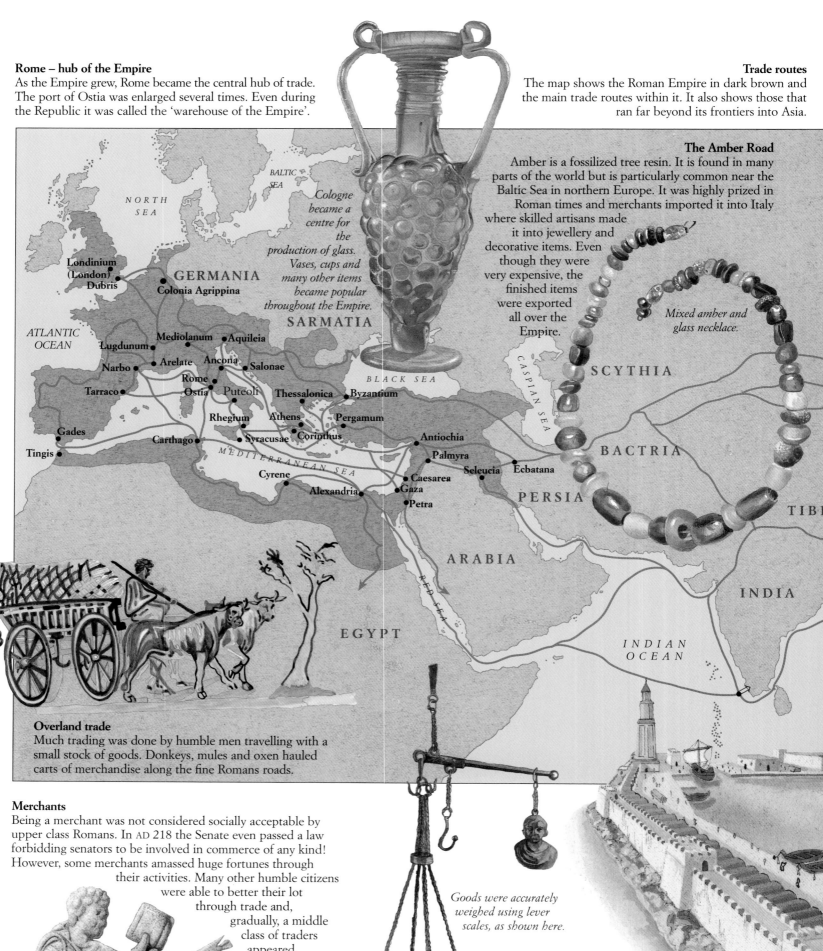

Rome – hub of the Empire

As the Empire grew, Rome became the central hub of trade. The port of Ostia was enlarged several times. Even during the Republic it was called the 'warehouse of the Empire'.

Trade routes

The map shows the Roman Empire in dark brown and the main trade routes within it. It also shows those that ran far beyond its frontiers into Asia.

The Amber Road

Amber is a fossilized tree resin. It is found in many parts of the world but is particularly common near the Baltic Sea in northern Europe. It was highly prized in Roman times and merchants imported it into Italy where skilled artisans made it into jewellery and decorative items. Even though they were very expensive, the finished items were exported all over the Empire.

Mixed amber and glass necklace.

Cologne became a centre for the production of glass. Vases, cups and many other items became popular throughout the Empire.

Overland trade

Much trading was done by humble men travelling with a small stock of goods. Donkeys, mules and oxen hauled carts of merchandise along the fine Romans roads.

Merchants

Being a merchant was not considered socially acceptable by upper class Romans. In AD 218 the Senate even passed a law forbidding senators to be involved in commerce of any kind! However, some merchants amassed huge fortunes through their activities. Many other humble citizens were able to better their lot through trade and, gradually, a middle class of traders appeared.

Sign advertising a bank shows the banker seated at his table.

Goods were accurately weighed using lever scales, as shown here.

Currency and payment

Trade within the Empire was made easy by the lack of frontiers, good roads and ports and the use of a single currency. The standard coin, called a *denarius*, was made of silver. During the late Republic and early Empire it was almost pure silver, but as the Empire's fortunes declined so did the purity of the silver.

Trade and Agriculture

Agriculture was the most important sector of the economy throughout Roman history. In early times the land was farmed by peasants who grew cereals, fruit and vegetables and raised a few animals on their tiny plots to keep themselves and their families. Gradually the land was taken over by wealthy landowners who established huge estates where peasants and slaves worked. They produced cereals, olive oil, wine, fruit and vegetables for local needs and, where possible, for export. Towns and cities all over the Empire imported large quantities of food to feed the urban population. Much of this food was sold in the city markets; some of it was distributed freely by the emperor or wealthy citizens in order to keep the poor people from starving. The main grain-producing areas were Sicily, Egypt and Africa, whereas most oil came from Spain or Africa. Many other goods were exported from one end of the Empire to the other. Growing cities, such as Rome, imported vast quantities of marble to build monuments. Wild animals, used in the gladitorial contests, were brought from outlying areas. Provinces rich in metals, linen or wool exported to those with scarcer resources. Luxury goods, such as incense, spices and silk, were carried vast distances from countries as far east as China and south-east Asia.

Painted pottery dish from China dating from the Han Dynasty (206 BC–AD 221). Trade with China began in Hellenistic times but increased in volume during the Republic and Empire.

The Silk Route
Silks imported from China travelled along the Silk Route through central Asia and into Europe. The Europeans sent wools, gold and silver back along the same road. The route was used until it became unsafe in the 13th–14th centuries.

Changan
Luoyang
CHINA

Ports and shipping
It was much cheaper, and faster, to move goods by sea or river routes than overland. Trading cities around natural or manmade harbours flourished. Herod the Great, king of Judaea, built the city of Caesarea (named in honour of Caesar Augustus, first Emperor of Rome), with its magnificent port Sebastos in the 1st century BC. Just fifteen days sailing from Rome, he hoped to make his city as large and powerful as Alexandria in Egypt.

Ships were towed into the harbour by tug boats. After ship's taxes had been collected, they anchored in the protected waters in front of the Temple of Augustus and Rome where they loaded and unloaded cargo.

Mercury, god of trade and merchants
The Roman god is identified with the Greek messenger god, Hermes. In Roman religion Mercury was the god of trade. He is usually shown holding a purse and staff and wearing a winged hat.

Roman trading ships
Amphorae (jars) or barrels containing olive oil, wine or fish sauce and sacks of grain were stored in the hull of merchant vessels. Trading ships came in all shapes and sizes, although the traditional Roman merchantman had a rounded hull, like the one being loaded here.

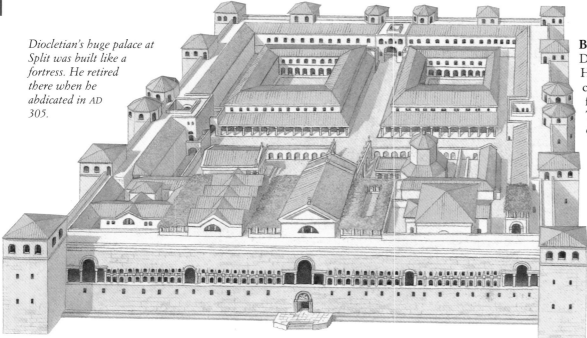

Diocletian's huge palace at Split was built like a fortress. He retired there when he abdicated in AD 305.

Buildings of the Late Empire
Diocletian had a limitless passion for building. He built splendid palaces for himself and his co-emperors, as well as houses for friends and family, mints, circuses, baths and factories. The cost was enormous and the Empire was constantly scoured for the workers and resources required. Diocletian's huge Baths in Rome had a frigidarium even larger than those of the Baths of Caracalla (see p. 7).

This colossal head of the Emperor Constantine was found in the Basilica Nova in Rome. It was originally part of an enormous seated statue.

The Late Empire and Christianity

The *Pax romana* (see pp. 42–43) was followed by almost a century of civil wars and constant attack by foreign invaders. The Empire was restored to some of its former glory in AD 284 when the Emperor Diocletian came to power. Diocletian increased the size of the army and strengthened frontier defences. He also reorganized the provinces, making them easier to control from central government. His most radical change was to introduce a system, called the tetrarchy, whereby four emperors ruled at the same time. He split the Empire into east and west and appointed a senior and a junior emperor to each part. The tetrarchy itself lasted only a few decades but it was an important step because it institutionalized the split of the Empire into East and West, preparing the way for the gradual division which occured in the 4th century. The reign of the Emperor Constantine marked another turning point in the history of the Empire. Constantine restored the power of a single emperor, made Christianity the official religion of the Empire and moved the centre of the Empire east to the city of Byzantium, which soon changed its name to Constantinople.

Constantine and Christianity
Constantine became western Emperor in 306. By 324 he had conquered his fellow emperor, reuniting the Empire under one man. He became a Christian in 312 after he had a vision of a flaming cross in the sky before winning the Battle of Milvian Bridge. He took a personal interest in church affairs, effectively linking Church and State in a way that would endure for centuries. Christianity gradually spread throughout the Empire.

The triumphal Arch of Constantine
Roman emperors often erected triumphal arches to commemorate victories. The Arch of Constantine, which still stands in the centre of Rome, was built to celebrate the Emperor's victory over Maxentius at Milvian Bridge. It was built quickly and was decorated with sculptural pieces from many older Roman monuments.

Division of the Empire into East and West

From the middle of the 3rd century AD the Empire was constantly invaded. The Persians attacked in the east and Germanic peoples in the north and west. In AD 260 the western provinces, alarmed by Rome's failure to defend them, broke away and formed their own Empire. The Gallic Empire only lasted for fifteen years but it set a precedent for the future.

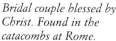

Map showing division of the Empire into East and West

Bridal couple blessed by Christ. Found in the catacombs at Rome.

Byzantine statue of the Emperors Diocletian and Maximian.

Persecutions

Diocletian insisted that everyone worship the traditional gods. Christianity had become a popular religion among soldiers and the middle classes. Imperial edicts ordered the destruction of churches, the burning of the scriptures and sacrifices to the pagan gods. Christians who refused these orders were murdered in their thousands.

Secret symbols of Christianity

An ancient symbol of Christianity, dating from the time of the persecutions, shows a cross and a fish. The Greek word for fish is *ichthys*; these are also the initials *Iesous Christos theou hyios soter* (Jesus Christ Son of God Saviour).

The catacombs

The catacombs were underground cemeteries. Early Christians used them to bury their dead. They also served as hiding places during the persecutions and later, to escape from the Barbarian invaders.

From joint rule to tetrarchy

Diocletian had to defend the Danube frontier and the western provinces. For this reason he appointed co-emperor Maximian and the two ruled jointly. He also appointed two junior emperors who would automatically succeed when he or Maximian abdicated or died.

Adoration of the Magi, 3rd century AD, from the catacombs at Rome.

Roman consul with charioteers dressed in the colours of four different factions.

The monastic movement

When Constantine made Christianity the official religion masses of people joined the Church. Disdainful, some original members withdrew to become hermits. The Syrian Simeon Stylites sat for thirty years on a pillar to resist the evil pleasures of the world. Here he is shown with a snake, representing worldly temptation.

Like Christianity, the Jewish religion was also introduced from the East. Jews were persecuted by the Romans as well.

The end of gladiatorial contests

Under Constantine new Christian principles outlawed the violent gladiatorial contests. These popular events were replaced by an increase in the number of chariot races at the circus.

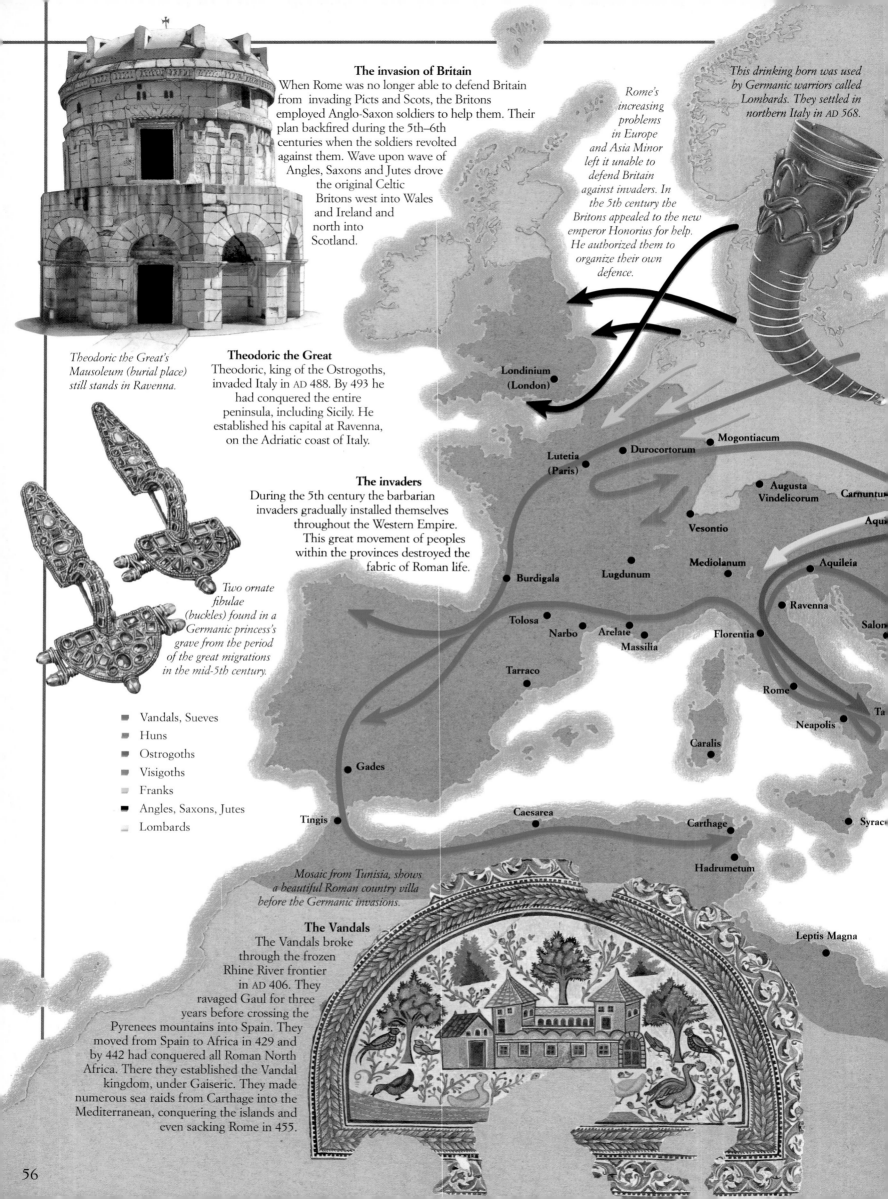

The invasion of Britain
When Rome was no longer able to defend Britain from invading Picts and Scots, the Britons employed Anglo-Saxon soldiers to help them. Their plan backfired during the 5th–6th centuries when the soldiers revolted against them. Wave upon wave of Angles, Saxons and Jutes drove the original Celtic Britons west into Wales and Ireland and north into Scotland.

Rome's increasing problems in Europe and Asia Minor left it unable to defend Britain against invaders. In the 5th century the Britons appealed to the new emperor Honorius for help. He authorized them to organize their own defence.

This drinking horn was used by Germanic warriors called Lombards. They settled in northern Italy in AD 568.

Theodoric the Great's Mausoleum (burial place) still stands in Ravenna.

Theodoric the Great
Theodoric, king of the Ostrogoths, invaded Italy in AD 488. By 493 he had conquered the entire peninsula, including Sicily. He established his capital at Ravenna, on the Adriatic coast of Italy.

The invaders
During the 5th century the barbarian invaders gradually installed themselves throughout the Western Empire. This great movement of peoples within the provinces destroyed the fabric of Roman life.

Two ornate fibulae (buckles) found in a Germanic princess's grave from the period of the great migrations in the mid-5th century.

- ▬ Vandals, Sueves
- ▬ Huns
- ▬ Ostrogoths
- ▬ Visigoths
- ▬ Franks
- ▬ Angles, Saxons, Jutes
- ▬ Lombards

Londinium (London)
Lutetia (Paris)
Durocortorum
Mogontiacum
Augusta Vindelicorum
Carnuntum
Vesontio
Aqui
Mediolanum
Aquileia
Burdigala
Lugdunum
Ravenna
Tolosa
Salon
Narbo
Arelate
Florentia
Massilia
Tarraco
Rome
Ta
Neapolis
Caralis
Gades
Caesarea
Tingis
Carthage
Syrac
Hadrumetum

Mosaic from Tunisia, shows a beautiful Roman country villa before the Germanic invasions.

Leptis Magna

The Vandals
The Vandals broke through the frozen Rhine River frontier in AD 406. They ravaged Gaul for three years before crossing the Pyrenees mountains into Spain. They moved from Spain to Africa in 429 and by 442 had conquered all Roman North Africa. There they established the Vandal kingdom, under Gaiseric. They made numerous sea raids from Carthage into the Mediterranean, conquering the islands and even sacking Rome in 455.

The Fall of the Empire

From around 200 AD more and more Germanic tribes began to raid the Empire. During the 3rd–4th centuries large numbers of them were settled within the frontiers. Many acted as mercenary soldiers for the Romans. Pressure on the northern borders mounted even further in the 4th century when the Huns first appeared in Europe. Originally from central Asia, the Huns migrated westwards during the 3rd–4th centuries. Their movement had a domino effect on the settled peoples in their path, who were pushed westwards before them. By the early 5th century Germanic tribes were pouring through the frontiers in numbers that the Romans were unable either to settle or turn back. The city of Rome was sacked by the Visigoths in AD 410. The Western Empire fell to the invaders in AD 476 when the last emperor abdicated.

Invaders and Romans
The Germanic invaders were always only a small minority in the areas they settled. They took control of government and divided the lands up among them. Lower class Romans and peasants were probably not much affected by the change.

Stilicho (above) was half-Roman and half-Vandal. He was one of the last great Roman military commanders and led several campaigns against the Visigoths and Ostrogoths.

The Byzantine Empire
Historians call the Eastern Roman Empire (after the fall of the West) the Byzantine Empire. With its capital at Constantinople, it survived for another 1,000 years, until it was toppled by the Turks in 1453.

From the 4th–6th centuries the Eastern emperors built many vast churches in the eastern Mediterranean. In Constantinople Justinian built the domed Santa Sophia (AD 532), the last great Roman building.

Sirmium

Constantinople

Thessalonica

Athens
Corinthus

Ephesus

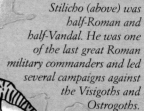

The Germanic tribes were not the only enemies of Rome. In the east the Parthians and Sassanians revived the Persian Empire (horseman above). Their raiding of the eastern frontiers required constant attention.

The Byzantine Emperor Justinian in a 6th century mosaic from the Church of San Vitale, Ravenna, Italy.

Cyrene

Justinian
When Justinian became Emperor of the Byzantine Empire in AD 518, the Western Empire was shattered. The Vandals held North Africa, the Franks ruled in Gaul and the Visigoths in Spain, while Britain had been abandoned to its fate long ago. Justinian's dream was to win the Empire back. He reconquered Africa in 533 and, after two decades of desperate fighting, Italy too. He was then forced by Persian attacks in the east to abandon his dream.

MAXIMIANVS

The Classical Legacy

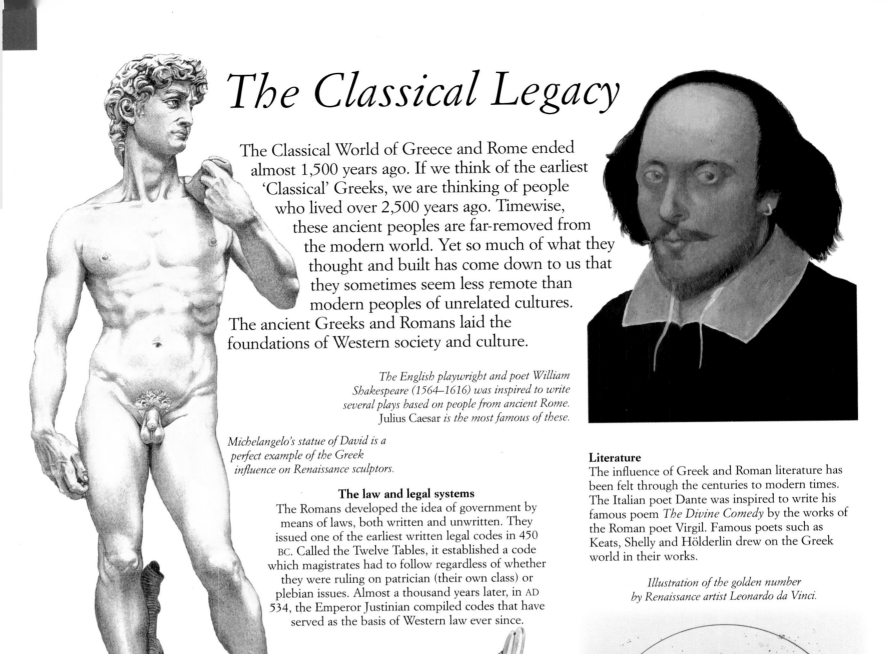

The Classical World of Greece and Rome ended almost 1,500 years ago. If we think of the earliest 'Classical' Greeks, we are thinking of people who lived over 2,500 years ago. Timewise, these ancient peoples are far-removed from the modern world. Yet so much of what they thought and built has come down to us that they sometimes seem less remote than modern peoples of unrelated cultures. The ancient Greeks and Romans laid the foundations of Western society and culture.

The English playwright and poet William Shakespeare (1564–1616) was inspired to write several plays based on people from ancient Rome. Julius Caesar *is the most famous of these.*

Michelangelo's statue of David is a perfect example of the Greek influence on Renaissance sculptors.

The law and legal systems
The Romans developed the idea of government by means of laws, both written and unwritten. They issued one of the earliest written legal codes in 450 BC. Called the Twelve Tables, it established a code which magistrates had to follow regardless of whether they were ruling on patrician (their own class) or plebian issues. Almost a thousand years later, in AD 534, the Emperor Justinian compiled codes that have served as the basis of Western law ever since.

Statue by Canova showing Cupid and Psyche *(1792). Many Neoclassical works of art depict themes from Greek or Roman mythology.*

The revival of Classical sculpture
During the Renaissance many Greek and Roman sculptures, such as the Laocoon group (see p. 29), were discovered. They were much studied by contemporary sculptors, such as Michelangelo and Donatello, who imitated their style and grace in their own works.

Neoclassicism
The Classical tradition did not die out after the Renaissance. It has reappeared many times since in sculpture, painting, architecture and thought. The artists who produce these works are often called Neoclassicists, because they imitate the Greeks and Romans.

Literature
The influence of Greek and Roman literature has been felt through the centuries to modern times. The Italian poet Dante was inspired to write his famous poem *The Divine Comedy* by the works of the Roman poet Virgil. Famous poets such as Keats, Shelly and Hölderlin drew on the Greek world in their works.

Illustration of the golden number by Renaissance artist Leonardo da Vinci.

The Golden Number
The Greeks were the first to express the idea of the golden number (1,617). It occurs when a rectangle is divided in two unequal parts and the ratio of the smaller part to the larger is the same as the larger part to the whole. According to Classical ideas, this is the perfect expression of proportion. They used it in architecture and other arts. Neoclassical artists have used it ever since.

The Greeks and scientific discovery

Ancient Greek thinkers made some fundamental contributions to scientific thought. Around 2,500 years ago, Democritus of Abdera stated that all matter was made up of particles, which he called 'atoms'. His idea was rejected as nonsense by great philosophers like Plato and Aristotle, but it was taken up by the Epicureans (a Greek philosophical school) and survived through the centuries until, substantially modified and elaborated, it was shown to be correct in modern times.

Modern scientists have kept many Greek words, like atom, out of respect for ancient thinkers who reached many correct or useful conclusions just by reasoning.

The Capitol in Washington, D.C., where the US Congress meets, recalls the Classical World in both appearance and function.

Alphabets and languages

Most of the modern languages of Europe, the Americas, Australasia and many other parts of the world are written using the Latin alphabet which the Latins adopted from the Etruscans in the 7th century BC. Modern languages derived directly from Latin include Spanish, French, Italian and Portuguese. The English language contains many words of Latin origin.

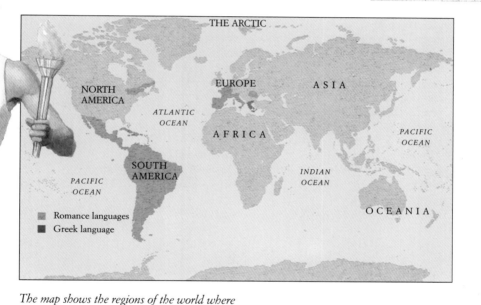

THE ARCTIC

NORTH AMERICA
ATLANTIC OCEAN
EUROPE
ASIA
AFRICA
PACIFIC OCEAN
SOUTH AMERICA
PACIFIC OCEAN
INDIAN OCEAN
OCEANIA

■ Romance languages
■ Greek language

The map shows the regions of the world where Romance languages and Greek are spoken.

The democractic ideal

Our word 'democracy' means rule by the people. Not surprisingly, it comes from two ancient Greek words – *demos*, meaning 'people' and *kratos*, meaning 'rule'. Democracy began in the city-states of ancient Greece more than 2,500 years ago. There was a gap of some 2,000 years between its disappearance there and its rise again in the modern world.

The Olympic flame is carried into the stadium during the opening ceremony of each Olympic Games. It is carried all the way from Olympia, Greece, to wherever the games are being held.

The Classical World and the Renaissance

The Renaissance (a word that means 'rebirth') began in Italy in the 13th century and gradually spread across Europe. It signalled the end of the Middle Ages and the birth of the modern world. During the Renaissance, artists, writers, scientists and philosophers studied the ancient Greeks and Romans with great interest. They tried to imitate the Ancient World by creating classical style buildings, sculptures, poems and art of all kinds.

The Olympic Games

The Olympics were held at Olympia once every four years until AD 393 when they were abolished by the Roman Emperor Theodosius I who, as a Christian, probably ojected to the pagan rites attached to the games. They were revived again in 1896, thanks to the efforts of Baron Pierre de Coubertin of France. The first modern Olympics were held in Athens. The Games have been held once every four years ever since (except during World War I and II) in various cities of the world. The Winter Olympics were introduced in 1924.

Raphael's great fresco The School of Athens is a typical Renaissance painting in the way it combines the ancient with the modern. The centre of the fresco shows Plato (pointing upwards) and Aristotle. Plato is actually a portrait of Leonardo da Vinci. Many other figures in the painting are also contemporaries of the artist.

Index

TIBERIUS

AUGUSTUS

NERO

CALIGULA

CLAUDIUS

VESPASIAN

TITUS

TRAJAN

DOMITIAN

HADRIAN

The Roman Emperors

27 BC-AD 14	Augustus
14-37	Tiberius
37-41	Caligula
41-54	Claudius
54-68	Nero
68-69	Galba
69	Otho
69	Vitellius
69-79	Vespasian
79-81	Titus
81-96	Domitian
96-98	Nerva
98-117	Trajan
117-138	Hadrian
138-161	Antoninus Pius
161-180	Marcus Aurelius
161-169	Lucius Verus
180-192	Commodus
193	Pertinax
193	Didius Julianus
193-211	Septimius Severus
211-217	Caracalla
211	Geta
217-218	Macrinus
218-222	Heliogabalus
222-235	Alexander Severus

235-238	Maximinus Thrax
238	Gordian I
238	Gordian II
238	Pupienus and Balbinus
238-244	Gordian III
244-249	Philip the Arab
249-251	Decius
251-253	Trebonianus Gallus
253	Aemilius Aemilianus
253-260	Valerian
253-268	Gallienus
268-270	Claudius II
270	Quintillus

The Gallic Empire
260-269	Postumus
269	Laelianus
269	Marius
268-271	Victorinus
271-274	Tetricus

The Palmyrene Empire
266-272	Zenobia

270-275	Aurelian
275-276	Tacitus
276	Florianus
276-282	Probus
282-283	Carus
283-284	Numerian
283-285	Carinus
284-286	Diocletian

*

WESTERN EMPIRE
286-305	Maximian
305-306	Constantius I
306-307	Severus II
306-312	Maxentius
307-324	Constantine the Great

*

EASTERN EMPIRE
286-305	Diocletian
305-311	Galerius
310-313	Maximinus Daia
308-324	Licinius
324-337	Constantine the Great

WESTERN EMPIRE
337-340	Constantine II
337-350	Constans I

*

EASTERN EMPIRE
337-361	Constantius II

*

361-363	Julian the Apostate
363-364	Jovian

*

WESTERN EMPIRE
364-375	Valentinian I
367-383	Gratian
375-392	Valentinian II
392-394	Eugenius
395-423	Honorius
423-425	Johannes
425-455	Valentinian III
455	Petronius Maximus
455-456	Avitus
457-461	Majorian
461-465	Severus III
467-472	Anthemius

472	Olybrius
473	Glycerius
474-475	Julius Nepos
475-476	Romulus Augustulus

*

EASTERN EMPIRE
364-378	Valens
379-395	Theodosius I
395-408	Arcadius
408-450	Theodosius II
450-457	Marcianus
457-474	Leo I
474	Leo II
474-491	Zeno
491-518	Anastasius
518-527	Justin I
527-565	Justinian I

The Eastern, or Byzantine, Empire lasted until 1453.